AWS Marketplace User Guide

A catalogue record for this book is available from the Hong Kong Public Libraries.

Published in Hong Kong by Samurai Media Limited.

Email: info@samuraimedia.org

ISBN 9789888408788

Contents

What is AWS Marketplace?

AWS Marketplace is an online store that helps customers find, buy, and immediately start using the software and services they need to build products and run their businesses. AWS Marketplace complements programs like the Amazon Partner Network and is another example of AWS's commitment to growing a strong ecosystem of software and solution partners.

Visitors to the marketplace can use AWS Marketplace's 1-Click deployment to quickly launch pre-configured software and pay only for what they use, by the hour or month. AWS handles billing and payments, and software charges appear on customers' AWS bill.

Topics

- How Can I Use AWS Marketplace?
- Additional Resources
- Getting Started as a Seller
- Preparing Your Product
- Submitting Your Listing for Publication
- AWS Marketplace Seller Reports
- Marketing Your Product

How Can I Use AWS Marketplace?

You use AWS Marketplace primarily as a subscriber (buyer), or as a seller.

Using AWS Marketplace as a Subscriber

AWS Marketplace is an online store where, as a subscriber, you can find, buy, and quickly deploy software that runs on Amazon Web Services (AWS). This software is available in the form of Amazon Machine Images (AMIs). An Amazon Machine Image (AMI) contains all the information necessary to boot an Amazon EC2 instance with your software. An EC2 instance is the virtual computing environment available from the Amazon Elastic Compute Cloud (Amazon EC2) web service.

An AMI is like a template of a computer's root volume. For example, an AMI might contain the software to act as a web server (Linux, Apache, and your web site) or it might contain the software to act as a Hadoop node (Linux, Hadoop, and a custom application). You can launch one or more EC2 instances from an AMI.

To buy software through AWS Marketplace, you subscribe to the software by purchasing a paid AMI, and then launch the software as an EC2 instance.

For more information, see the following topics in the* Amazon EC2 User Guide for Linux Instances*:

- Finding a Paid AMI
- Purchasing a Paid AMI
- Launching an AWS Marketplace Instance
- Managing Your AWS Marketplace Subscriptions

Using AWS Marketplace as a Seller

As a seller, you can build a custom AMI to sell on AWS Marketplace and manage the sales channel for products you sell. For information about becoming a seller on AWS Marketplace, go to the AWS Marketplace Management Portal. For detailed information about selling your AMI, see Selling Your AMI in the *Amazon EC2 User Guide for Linux Instances.*

To manage the sales channel for products you sell on AWS Marketplace, you use the AWS Marketplace Management Portal, where you can access five different pages from the navigation bar links:

- **Marketing page**

  Use this page to view the results of your marketing efforts and to better understand the traffic, conversion, customer usage, and revenue that your marketing efforts generate.

- **Customer Support Eligibility page**

  Your support staff can use this page to access near-real-time information about a customer's subscription to your products and provide fast, personalized service.

- **Reports page**

  Use this page to download all your latest reports, including Weekly Ref Tag Reports and other product subscription and usage reports.

- **Manage Products page**

  Use this page to share your AMI with AWS Marketplace and have your AMI scanned to ensure it meets the listing requirements. You can also view all your AMIs (whether shared or unshared), and download data for your existing published products.

- **File Upload page**

  Use this page to upload files to AWS Marketplace, including product metadata, images, and product documentation.

Additional Resources

For more information about how to work with AWS Marketplace and AWS Marketplace Management Portal, including how AWS manages billing for AWS Marketplace products, how to get support for products you purchase on AWS Marketplace, and where AWS Marketplace fits in with Amazon DevPay or the AWS Partner Network, see the AWS Marketplace Help and FAQ.

Getting Started as a Seller

If you are interested in selling your software on AWS Marketplace, review the requirements, and then follow the steps to register as a seller. There are different registration requirements based on where you reside and what type of products you want to list. To register as a seller on AWS Marketplace, you can use an existing AWS account or create a new account. All AWS Marketplace interactions will be tied to the AWS account you choose.

Seller Requirements for Publishing Free Products on AWS Marketplace

- Sell publicly available, full-feature production-ready software (not a beta product).
- Have a defined customer support process and support organization.
- Provide a means to keep software regularly updated and free of vulnerabilities.
- Follow best practices and guidelines when marketing your product on AWS Marketplace.
- Be an AWS customer in good standing and meet the requirements set forth in the terms and conditions for AWS Marketplace sellers.

Additional Seller Requirements for Publishing Paid or BYOL Products on AWS Marketplace

- Be a permanent U.S. or European Union (EU) resident or citizen, or a business entity organized or incorporated in the United States or member state of the EU.
- Tax and bank account information are required. For U.S. based entities, a W-9 and banking account from a U.S. based bank are required.
- European Union state members are required to provide a W-8, Value Added Tax (VAT) number, and U.S. bank account. If you do not have a U.S. bank account, you can register for a virtual U.S. bank account from Hyperwallet.

To sell into the AWS GovCloud (US) Region, sellers must have an AWS GovCloud account. For details on ITAR requirements, refer to the AWS GovCloud (US) User Guide.

Contact the **AWS Marketplace Seller Operations** (aws-marketplace-seller-ops@amazon.com) team with any questions on AWS Marketplace seller requirements or the registration process.

AWS Marketplace Management Portal (AMMP)

The AWS Marketplace Management Portal is the tool you use to register as an AWS Marketplace seller, and then to manage the products you list on AWS Marketplace. You can:

- Register as an AWS Marketplace Seller.
- Use the Self-Service Listings interface to submit new, and update existing products.
- Monitor the status of your requests.
- Upload files needed to create and manage your new listings.
- Manage your listing into incremental channel revenue by taking advantage of the go-to-market activities.
- Measure the results of your marketing efforts within hours of launch, including the usage and revenue driven by your campaigns.
- Customer service representatives can retrieve customer data in real-time.
- Access AMI Self-Sharing to scan your AMI's for vulnerabilities.

All registered sellers can access the AMMP using their AWS credentials for the account used to list their products (the Seller of Record). If you need help determining the specific account that is the Seller of Record for your products, contact the **AWS Marketplace Seller Operations** team (aws-marketplace-seller-ops@amazon.com).

AWS Marketplace **STRONGLY** recommends using IAM roles to sign in to the Management Portal rather than using your root account credentials. See Create IAM Users for details.

The AMMP is always evolving and we welcome any and all feedback on your experience using the AWS Marketplace Management Portal. Send feedback to **ammp-feedback@amazon.com**.

Seller Registration Process

To register as an AWS Marketplace seller, from the AWS Marketplace Management Portal (AMMP), choose **Sign Up as an AWS Marketplace Seller** and follow the wizard to complete registration. Identify an AWS account to use as your primary AWS Marketplace account. You can use an existing account or register a new AWS Account so long as the account is linked to a valid payment method. This account will be the seller of record for your products on AWS Marketplace and will be used for reporting, disbursement and communication from the AWS Marketplace to you.

NOTE: Once you use an AWS account to list a product on AWS Marketplace, you cannot change the AWS account associated with the product.

You can change other product information (name, website, description) on AWS Marketplace once the product is listed. You can also use AWS Identity and Access Management (AWS IAM) to configure your primary AWS account to allow multiple users with various permissions to access the AMMP. For more information visit Controlling User Access to the AWS Marketplace Management Portal.

U.S. Bank Account for European Union State Member Sellers

A U.S. bank account is required for EU based sellers that wish to sell paid software in AWS Marketplace. AWS Marketplace only disburses to U.S. bank accounts. If you do not already have a U.S. bank account, you may be able to obtain one through Hyperwallet. Hyperwallet can provide you with a U.S. account, which you can provide to AWS Marketplace for your AWS Marketplace disbursements.

Hyperwallet is an independent service provider that may enable you to transfer funds to a European (or other) bank account in a supported currency. For a limited time, you will not be required to pay certain Hyperwallet service fees in connection with AWS Marketplace disbursements.

- By adding your Hyperwallet account details to your AWS Marketplace seller account, you agree and acknowledge that AWS Marketplace will share your name, email address and account number with Hyperwallet to confirm your status as an AWS Marketplace seller.
- Additional fees may apply to your use of Hyperwallet services (including transfer fees and foreign exchange fees required to transfer funds into your local currency), as well as foreign exchange rates. Hyperwallet's service fee will be waived for a limited time, and only with respect to AWS Marketplace disbursements of the proceeds from your Paid Listings into your Hyperwallet account. Consult the Fees section of the Hyperwallet site or contact Hyperwallet for more information and to review applicable fees.

To begin registration with Hyperwallet and obtain your U.S. bank account information:

1. Use the URL and PIN emailed to you by AWS Marketplace to register with Hyperwallet. You will receive the email as part of your registration process.

2. Once you have activated your Hyperwallet account, follow the steps described on the Hyperwallet registration portal to complete registration and receive your deposit account information.

3. When you have obtained an account from Hyperwallet, add your Hyperwallet account information to your AWS account using the Bank Account Registration Tool.

U.S. Sales and Use Tax

AWS Marketplace Tax Calculation Service provides the ability to calculate and collect U.S. sales and use tax for existing and new products. Some states are not eligible for Tax Calculation Service because AWS Marketplace is required by law to collect and remit applicable sales tax attributable to taxable sales of your product(s) to customers based in these states. To use the service, configure your tax nexus settings for your seller profile, and then assign product tax codes to your products.

To configure your tax nexus settings, open the AWS Marketplace Management Portal (AMMP), and under the **Settings** tab configure the applicable tax nexus settings. Then, assign product tax codes (PTCs) to your products through the Self-Service Listings dashboard. We recommend you review the AWS Marketplace Tax Methodology and AWS Marketplace Product Tax Code Guidance in their entirety prior to completing this process., For product types not supported by Self Service Listings, you will need to download and edit a https://s3.amazonaws.com/awsmp-loadforms/ProductDataLoad-Current.xlsx.

Once you have completed these two steps, U.S. sales and use tax calculation will be enabled for new products that do not have any subscribers. For products that have existing subscribers, tax calculation will not start until after AWS Marketplace gives subscribers at least 90 days' notice of the change. Please note:

- Activation of your tax nexus settings takes from five to 48 hours.
- Tax nexus settings must be configured before you can assign PTCs.
- PTC assignment happens 24 hours after the AWS Marketplace team approves and publishes your product listing, which may take 3-5 days from the time you submit your listing change request. For details, please refer to section 2.2 of this document.
- For products with existing subscribers, no customers (existing or new) will be charged taxes until after the 90 days' notice of change. Then, all customers of the product are charged U.S. Sales and Use Tax where applicable.
- When tax calculation begins, estimated sales tax charges will be included in customer invoices. Sales tax will be calculated based on factors including, but not limited to, the customer's billing address, the tax code of your product listing, and your tax nexus settings. The resulting sales tax charge, if applicable, will be included in the customer's invoice and identified as a US sales tax charge under the specific product sold by your company. Please note that customer invoices will show your company's Legal Name, which you provided when you registered to become an AWS Marketplace seller.
- The collected sales tax funds are sent with your monthly disbursement, and the U.S. Sales and Use Tax Report is available to you on the 15th of the month, detailing what taxes were collected. You are responsible for remitting your own taxes.

If you enroll for the AWS Marketplace Tax Calculation Service, we also recommend that you register for the Amazon Tax Exemption Program (ATEP). You are not required to use this service; however, we recommend that all AWS Marketplace sellers who use the Tax Calculation Service participate in ATEP to help reduce the number of tax-only refunds that will need to be processed to qualified customers registered in ATEP.

You can edit or delete the tax nexus information you have added at any time by navigating back to the Tax Calculation Service Settings page in AMMP and making the changes you desire.

Value-added Tax (VAT)

Please be advised that Amazon Web Services is required to charge value added taxes (VAT) on your AWS Marketplace sales of electronically supplied services to private (non-business) European Union customers, per application of Article 9a of Council Regulation n. 282/2011 of 15 March 2011 & Article 28 of Directive 2006/112/EC. VAT collected will be remitted by AWS to the tax authority of the appropriate EU member state.

France

Please be advised that you that you could potentially be liable to French taxing authorities for taxes and social security contributions on transactions from/with/in France. To help you comply with any potential French tax obligations, a new monthly Tax Disclosure Report listing your France sales transactions, on your AWS Marketplace sales of electronically supplied services to customers located in France, will be sent to you on or about the 15th of each month. Your annual Tax Disclosure Report will be made available to you no later than the January 31st of each year. For more information, please consult the French authorities' websites or your tax advisor:

- https://www.impots.gouv.fr/portail/node/10841
- http://www.securite-sociale.fr/Vos-droits-et-demarches-dans-le-cadre-des-activites-economiques-entre-particuliers-Article-87

Japan

There has been a reassessment of the tax treatment of cross border digital services based on the 2015 Japan Tax Reform. As a result, AWS Marketplace sellers may have Japan consumption tax obligations for sales to customers in Japan. If you sell any software through AWS Marketplace to a customer in Japan (business or individual), you may now have to pay tax. Anyone whose billing address is in Japan is considered a customer in Japan in this case. We recommend that you consult with your tax advisor to determine whether you have tax obligations in connection with this reassessment.

Disbursement

- A valid Payment Method, a Registered U.S. bank account and a submitted W9 form are required for disbursement.
- AWS disburses payments monthly directly to the bank account associated with the seller account, less AWS Marketplace service fees. Payment is disbursed on a rolling monthly basis based off of when the seller account was created, not the beginning of each month.
- Funds are disbursed only after they are collected from the customer.
- If you participate in the AWS Marketplace Tax Calculation Service, any U.S. Sales and Use Tax collected from customers will be included in your monthly disbursement.

Already a Seller?

Manage your listing into incremental channel revenue by taking advantage of the go-to-market activities made available in the AWS Marketplace Management Portal.

- Measure the results of your marketing efforts within hours, including the usage and revenue driven by your campaigns
- Customer service representatives can retrieve customer data in real-time
- Upload files needed to create and manage your listing and monitor progress as we process them

AWS Marketplace Commerce Analytics Service

The AWS Marketplace Commerce Analytics service allows you to programmatically access product and customer data through AWS Marketplace.

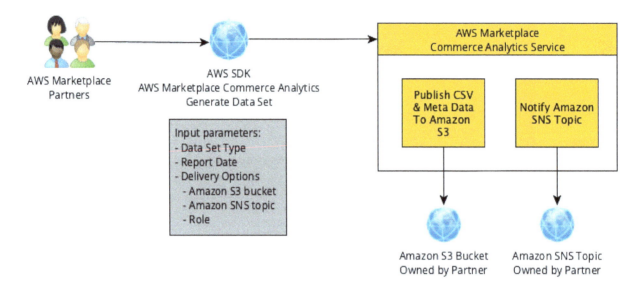

Data is delivered as data sets. Most of the data sets correspond the same data as the text-based reports available on the AWS Marketplace Management Portal (AMMP). You can request data sets for a specific date, and the data will be delivered to the provided Amazon S3 bucket. Notification of data delivery is provided by the Amazon Simple Notification Service (SNS).

Terms and Conditions

These AWS Marketplace Commerce Analytics Service Terms and Conditions (these "**CAS Terms**") contain the terms and conditions specific to your use of and access to the AWS Marketplace Commerce Analytics Service ("**CA Service**") and are effective as of the date you click an "I Accept" button or check box presented with these CAS Terms or, if earlier, when you use any CA Service offerings. These CAS Terms are an addendum to the Terms and Conditions for AWS Marketplace Sellers (the "**Marketplace Seller Terms**") between you and Amazon Web Services, Inc. ("**AWS**," "**we**," "**us**" or "**our**"), the terms of which are hereby incorporated herein. In the event of a conflict between these CAS Terms and the Marketplace Seller Terms, the terms and conditions of these CAS Terms apply, but only to the extent of such conflict and solely with respect to your use of the CA Service. Capitalized terms used herein but not defined herein shall have the meanings set forth in the Marketplace Seller Terms.

1. **CA Services and CAS Data.** To qualify for access to the CA Service you must be an AWS Marketplace Seller bound by existing Marketplace Seller Terms. Information and data you receive or have access to in connection with the CA Service ("**CAS Data**") constitutes Subscriber Information and is subject to the restrictions and obligations set forth in the Marketplace Seller Terms. You may use CAS Data on a confidential basis to improve and target marketing and other promotional activities related to Your Marketplace Content provided that you do not (a) disclose CAS Data to any third party; (b) use any CAS Data in any way inconsistent with applicable privacy policies or law; (c) contact a subscriber to influence them to make an alternative purchase outside of the AWS Marketplace; (d) disparage us, our affiliates or any of their or our respective products; or (e) target communications of any kind on the basis of the intended recipient being an AWS Marketplace subscriber.

2. **CA Service Limitations and Security.** You will only access (or attempt to access) the CA Service by the means described in the CA Service documentation. You will not misrepresent or mask your identity or

your client's identity when using the CA Service. We reserve the right, in our sole discretion, to set and enforce limits on your use of the CA Service, including, without limitation, with respect to the number of connections, calls and servers permitted to access the CA Service during any period of time. You agree to, and will not attempt to circumvent such limitations. We reserve the right to restrict, suspend or terminate your right to access the CA Service if we believe that you may be in breach of these CAS Terms or are misusing the CA Service.

3. **CA Service Credential Confidentiality and Security.** CA Service credentials (such as passwords, keys and client IDs) are intended to be used by you to identify your API client. You are solely responsible for keeping your credentials confidential and will take all reasonable measures to avoid disclosure, dissemination or unauthorized use of such credentials, including, at a minimum, those measures you take to protect your own confidential information of a similar nature. CA Service credentials may not be embedded on open source projects. You are solely responsible for any and all access to the CA Service with your credentials.

4. **Modification.** We may modify these CAS Terms at any time by posting a revised version on the AWS Site or providing you with notice in accordance with the Marketplace Seller Terms. The modified terms will become effective upon posting or, if we notify you by email, as stated in the email message. By continuing use or access the CA Service after the effective date of any modifications to these CAS Terms, you agree to be bound by the modified terms.

5. **Termination.** These CAS Terms and the rights to use CAS Data granted herein will terminate, with or without notice to you upon termination of your Marketplace Seller Terms for any reason. In addition, we may stop providing the CA Services or terminate your access to the CA Services at any time for any or no reason.

AWS Marketplace Enhanced Data Sharing Program

The AWS Marketplace (AWSMP) Enhanced Data Sharing (EDS) program focuses on delivering "enhanced" buyer information, such as buyer email domain, AWS Account ID, and location, on a daily and monthly basis to select AWS Marketplace Sellers. The goal of delivering buyer information is to provide a framework for AWSMP Sellers to compensate their sales teams for AWSMP subscription revenue. Sharing monthly billed revenue information, usage information, and disbursed funds information by buyer provides a mechanism to help you correctly map deals and opportunities to the appropriate sales representative by company, geography and AWS Account ID.

Requirements for AWS Marketplace Seller Participation

This program requires that the data only be used to activate and motivate AWS Marketplace Seller field sales via formal sales compensation plans. For more information regarding the program and instructions on how to enroll, contact aws-marketplace-seller-ops@amazon.com. Enrollment requirements include:

1. **Annual pricing** on all of your AWS Marketplace product listings
2. **Sales compensation plans for all AWSMP subscription revenue** (hourly, monthly, annual, or metering)
3. **Formal announcement of AWSMP compensation plan **
4. **Agreement to treat EDS data as confidential information** and not distribute it for the purposes of lead-generation

Benefits for AWS Marketplace Sellers

Benefits of enrolling in EDS include:

1. It increases the collective number of sales reps driving awareness and adoption of AWSMP subscriptions for your products.
2. It provides incentive and compensation to your sales reps working with AWS customers and prospects.
3. It provides you with customer data to assist in analyzing, growing and compensating sales teams for AWSMP sell-through.
4. It fosters a collaborative working relationship between AWS Sales and your sales team to better address customer needs.

Sales Compensation Report: Contents, Timing, and Delivery

The EDS program offers a Sales Compensation report which provides buyer data (email domain, AWS Account ID, and location) in conjunction with monthly billed revenue. The Sales Compensation report is available on the 15th of each month and can be downloaded in the AWS Marketplace Management Portal (AMMP) or by using the AWS Marketplace Commerce Analytics Service (CAS) API.

In addition, sellers that are enrolled in EDS automatically receive additional buyer data columns including email domain, AWS Account ID, and location across their key seller reports, including:

- The Daily Business Report (available every 24 hours)
- The Monthly Billed Revenue Report (available on the 15th of each month)
- The Disbursement Report (available monthly between the 10th and 13th of the month, depending on the seller)

By adding sales compensation data to your normal reports, the EDS program enables you to compensate your team on a daily basis, at the time of disbursement, or at the time of billing. If you compensate your team based on the Daily Business Report, please note that this report reflects estimated usage.

Sales Compensation Report Contents

The Sales Compensation Report contains the following fields; for details regarding each Sales Compensation Report field, refer to the Sales Compensation Report documentation.

- Payer AWS Account ID
- Payer Country
- Payer State
- Payer Zip Code
- Payer Email Domain
- Product Code
- Product Title
- Gross Revenue
- AWS Revenue Share
- Gross Refunds
- AWS Refunds Share
- Net Revenue
- Currency
- AR Period
- Transaction Reference ID

Sales Compensation Report Timing

The Sales Compensation Report is available on the 15th of each month. Within the report, the timing of each line item differs based on the subscription type, as outlined below:

- *Hourly Subscriptions* are billed between the 1st and 5th of the month following usage, and are reported in in the Sales Compensation Report within 2 months of the usage date. For example, January hourly usage would be billed to customers in February and would appear on your Sales Compensation Report issued in March. (Note: This report timing also applies to SaaS Subscriptions products and products with Usage-based pricing.)
- *Monthly Subscriptions* are billed at the beginning of each month between the 1st and 5th of the month following usage, and are reported in the Sales Compensation Report within 1 month of the usage date. For example, you would see January monthly usage in your February Sales Compensation Report.
- *Annual Subscriptions* are billed on the purchase date, and are reported in the Sales Compensation Report within 1 month of the transaction date. For example, an annual subscription purchase in January would appear in your February Sales Compensation Report.

Sales Compensation Report Delivery

For AWS Marketplace Sellers enrolled in the EDS program, the Sales Compensation report is available on the 15th of each month and can be downloaded in the AWS Marketplace Management Portal (AMMP) or by using the AWS Marketplace Commerce Analytics Service (CAS) API. You will be notified by email when your report is available for download each month. The notification is sent to the email address associated with your AWS Account.

Use of the Data

The information shared with you as part of this program constitutes Amazon's Confidential Information under our nondisclosure agreement with you or, if no such agreement exists, the Terms and Conditions for AWS Marketplace Sellers. The purpose of our sharing this information is to allow you to evaluate the effectiveness of your marketing campaigns and communicate commission payments to your employees. You may use such information for the foregoing purpose, including by sharing such information with employees who have a need to know such information to understand the source of commissions payable to them, provided that your use and sharing of such information complies with the confidentiality obligations in the agreements specified above, including, without limitation, Section 3.8 of the Terms and Conditions for AWS Marketplace Sellers.

EDS Program FAQs

By participating in the EDS program, will I receive an identifiable corporate email domain for every customer?

Not necessarily. The Sales Compensation Report that you receive will contain the email domain that the customer shared with AWS. In some cases, this domain may be a generic email domain associated with a personal email address, as opposed to an identifiable corporate email domain.

Does the Sales Compensation Report contain billed revenue or disbursed revenue?

The Sales Compensation Report contains buyer information with monthly billed revenue

I prefer to compensate my field based on disbursed revenue, not billed revenue. How can I map the Sales Compensation Report to my disbursed revenue?

AWSMP issues a Disbursement Report each month for every seller with paid product listings; this report covers all disbursed revenue for the month and is available through both AWS Marketplace Management Portal (AMMP) and via the AWS Marketplace Commerce Analytics Service (CAS) API. By participating in EDS, you will also receive additional customer data columns (email domain, location, and AWS account ID) directly in your monthly Disbursement Report.

I prefer to compensate my field based on daily usage data. How can I do this?

As an EDS participant, you will automatically receive additional customer data columns, including email domain, location, and AWS Account ID, in your Daily Business Report, which is published every 24 hours and is available through both AMMP and the CAS API.

How does the timing of the Sales Compensation Report relate to the timing of the Disbursement Report that I receive from AWSMP?

The Sales Compensation Report is available in AMMP and via the CAS API on the 15th day of each month. Disbursement Reports are typically published between the 10th and 13th of each month. For questions regarding your specific Disbursement Report delivery schedule, please contact aws-marketplace-seller-ops@amazon.com.

How does the timing of the Sales Compensation Report relate to the timing of the Monthly Billed Revenue Report that I receive from AWSMP?

The Sales Compensation Report and Monthly Billed Revenue Report are both published on the 15th day of each month and contain information regarding monthly billed revenue. The Monthly Billed Revenue Report does not include identifiable customer data; line items from these two reports can be cross-referenced using the Transaction Reference ID.

Product Support Connection

Product Support Connection

AWS Marketplace Product Support Connection (PSC) is a feature that allows AWS Marketplace customers to provide contact information in the AWS Marketplace website for the purposes of obtaining and accessing product support from AWS Marketplace Sellers. AWS Marketplace shares the provided data with participating Sellers via an API to enable a better support experience. Customers can choose to add contact details during or after a purchase of PSC-enabled AWS Marketplace products, and Sellers can retrieve the Customer contact data, along with relevant product subscription details, by calling a pull-based API.

Your staff can use the Customer Support Eligibility tool to access near-real-time information about a customer's subscription to your products and provide fast, personalized service. AWS Marketplace Management Portal makes it easy to get started: enter a customer's AWS account ID to retrieve subscription and usage information from their account.

You also have the option to enroll your products in AWS Marketplace Product Support Connection (PSC). For products that are enrolled in PSC, AWS Marketplace customers can choose to provide contact information (including name, organization, email address, and phone number) via the AWS Marketplace web site for the purposes of obtaining and accessing product support. If you enroll in PSC, AWS Marketplace will share the provided data with you via an API to help enable a more seamless support experience.

How does AWS Marketplace Product Support Connection benefit me as a Seller?

Participating in PSC can make it easier for you to provide support to customers that subscribe to your products on AWS Marketplace. The data available through the program lets you keep customer contact information up to date in your support or CRM system(s). If an AWS Marketplace customer shares contact information through PSC and then contacts you for support, you will be able to quickly access and verify the customer's identity and product subscription details.

What information will AWS Marketplace Product Support Connection collect from customers?

We collect first and last name, job title, company name, email address, telephone number, country, and zip code. Providing contact details is optional, but if a customer chooses to provide contact details, then organization, first and last name, email, and telephone number are required fields. All provided details, along with the customer's AWS account number, product ID, product code, and subscription start date, are available to participating Sellers via a pull-based API. Customers can add information for up to 5 contacts per product subscription, and they can also edit or delete their contact details later.

Will I receive contact details for every customer subscribed to my product?

Not necessarily. Entering and sharing contact information is optional for customers, although we recommend that customers share at least one contact for supported products in order to receive a better product support experience.

At what point in the purchase process does a customer become eligible for PSC?

Customers have the option to provide contact details for PSC during or after a subscription to a PSC-enabled product. For AMI-based products, customers that choose Annual or Monthly subscription options are charged for the product when they subscribe; customers that choose hourly subscriptions are charged when they launch an instance. For more information about what it means for customers to subscribe to a product, please visit the AWS Marketplace Help Pages.

Will I receive data about a customer's product usage?

No; at this time, PSC collects contact details and subscription information only. Usage data is not currently collected as part of this program.

Seller Requirements

What do I need to do to qualify to participate in AWS Marketplace Product Support Connection?

To participate, there are specific policies you must follow:

- You must list commercially supported, enterprise production versions of your software with a dedicated support email address (or equivalent contact method) that is usable by customers and AWS Customer Support.
- You must compensate your sales force for all AWS Marketplace transactions that occur in a sales territory or named account segment. Communication on AWS Marketplace compensation must be sent to your Global Field, and AWS must receive a copy of that communication.
- Your Customer Support teams must outline a policy regarding how you plan to provide support for AWS Marketplace customers, and should provide AWS Marketplace with a copy of your policy. This guidance must be provided to your Customer Support teams in order for AWS Marketplace to engage with your Customer Support.
- Any customer information provided to you through the API should be added to your systems within one business day. In addition, customers must have the ability to opt out of the program at any time. The data available through the PSC API will indicate when a customer has deleted contact details and wishes to be removed from the program.

If you have any questions about these program requirements, please reach out to the AWS Marketplace Seller Operations team at aws-mp-seller-ops@amazon.com.

What steps do I need to complete in order to participate in Product Support Connection?

You must complete the following steps in order to participate:

1. Using the static test dataset that is available, integrate with the PSC API so that data provided through the API will be added to your backend CRM or support system(s) within no more than one business day. See "Integrating with the Seller API" and "Handling Customer Data" below for more details.

2. Provide a list of the product(s) you would like to enroll in the program to the AWS Marketplace team (aws-marketplace-seller-ops@amazon.com). This will ensure that your products are flagged for enrollment in PSC. See "Enrolling Your Products" below for more details.

3. Work with the AWS Marketplace team to ensure that your product detail pages contain a valid support email address or equivalent contact method.

4. Provide a description (about 1 page) of the support processes you plan to follow for AWS Marketplace customers, and submit your description to aws-marketplace-seller-ops@amazon.com. This description should outline your planned support processes in a few paragraphs and should be provided to AWS Marketplace in addition to being communicated to your internal support team. This document is for AWS Marketplace internal use and helps us track the customer experience across products that are enrolled in PSC. See below for a list of questions your writeup should address.

5. You can optionally customize your Welcome email, which customers receive after subscribing to your product, to describe your PSC support processes or give your customers more information about product support. Please reach out to aws-marketplace-seller-ops@amazon.com if you wish to customize your Welcome email content.

What information should I include in my description of support processes?

- Which product listing(s) will you enroll in PSC?
- Have you already built and tested a way to pull data from the API and port it to your support systems?
- If yes, please describe how you import this data to your support systems?
- If no, when do you expect to have this implemented? Please describe your planned approach.
- Please summarize your support process for AWS Marketplace customers that participate in PSC.
- How can AWS Marketplace PSC customers contact you to receive support for these products (email, phone, other methods)?
- If PSC customers contact you for support, how long will it typically take before they receive a reply?
- Do you have different support levels for different AWS Marketplace products? If so, please describe your support tiers and what they cover.
- What communications do you plan to send to customers under your support policy? If you plan to send proactive communications, please describe what you plan to send.
- After customers enter their data in the AWS Marketplace site, how long will it take for the data to appear in your support system(s)?
- If a customer opts out of PSC, what is your process for deleting their contact data?
- Do you have a web page describing the support you offer for AWS Marketplace customers? If so, please provide it.

Enrolling Your Products

How do I enroll products in PSC?

After reviewing the program requirements, contact the AWS Marketplace Seller Catalog Operations team to provide a list of the products you would like to enroll in PSC. You can enroll new or existing AMI-based product listings in the program. Please allow 1-2 weeks for your request to be processed. You will need to verify that you have completed integration with the API before your products can be enabled for PSC. As described above, you must also provide a valid support email address on your product listing page(s), and you should provide a writeup describing the data handling and support process you plan to follow for AWS Marketplace customers.

Handling Customer Data

How can I use the data available through Product Support Connection?

Information you receive under the PSC program constitutes "Subscriber Information" under the Terms and Conditions for AWS Marketplace Sellers (the "Seller Terms") and may only be used in accordance with the Seller Terms (including Section 3.8 thereof). The data cannot be used for marketing or other purposes not related to product support.

How should I handle and store customer data provided through AWS Marketplace Product Support Connection?

You must handle customer data in accordance with applicable law and your privacy policy; we recommend that customer data should be encrypted in transit and at rest. The provided customer data constitutes Subscriber Information under the Seller Terms and can only be used for providing product support.

Preparing Your Product

You prepare your product for publication on AWS Marketplace by configuring your package, setting a pricing scheme, determining what categories your product should show under, and adding keywords so your product appears in relevant searches.

Your product can be an AMI-based product, or a software as a service (SaaS) product. Each has several options for packaging, pricing and delivery. Some product types are not available to you as a seller on AWS Marketplace until you register for the program supporting that product type.

AWS Marketplace Private Offers

AWS Marketplace Private Offers is a purchasing program that allows an AWS Marketplace buyer and an AWS Marketplace seller to negotiate a custom price and End User Licensing Agreement (EULA) terms when purchasing products available on AWS Marketplace. Enterprise Contract Private Offers will use the Enterprise Contract EULA. To register for Private Offers, sellers first must enroll in the AWS Enhanced Data Sharing program.

Interested in registering or learning more about Private Offers? Work with your AWS Marketplace Business Development point of contact, or contact the AWS Marketplace Customer Desk (mpcustdesk@amazon.com) to register for the Private Offers program.

AWS Marketplace Custom Private Offers

AWS Marketplace Custom Private Offers If you are unable to create a private offer to your required , the AWS Marketplace Customer Desk can help. AWS Marketplace Custom Private Offers are offers that are manually published by the AWS Marketplace Business Development (BD) Operations team. This process must be used to create private offers for BYOL products, non-standard invoicing and other situations. The steps to process each Custom Private Offer type are different.

Once you have initiated contact, the team will contact you if they need information specific to your private offer request. To initiate a custom private offer, email the AWS Marketplace Customer Desk team, or work with your Customer Advisor or Business Development contact to request a custom private offer. The team will email you instructions, including forms that you and/or the buyer must complete and return. After you have returned the completed forms, the team will complete the publication of your private offer.

The process takes from 5-7 business days from first contact with AWS Marketplace. When your private offer is published on AWS Marketplace, the AWS Marketplace Customer Desk team will email you a link to the private offer and the offer will be visible to the buyer in their AWS Marketplace Management portal.

The following product types are currently not supported for Private Offers: 2P, SaaS Redirect, and CARMA. Contact the AWS Marketplace Customer Desk (mpcustdesk@amazon.com) for additional information.

AMI-Based Products

AMI is the acronym for Amazon Machine Image.

Product ID and Product Codes

Each product in AWS Marketplace is assigned a unique product ID which is used to track and identify the product in our catalog, and is included in seller reports. A unique product code is assigned to all AMIs submitted to AWS Marketplace. The unique product ID is used to distinguish your product in AWS Marketplace, provide access to users who purchase your product, as well as for the customer billing process.

Sellers can obtain the Product Code while developing their software so it can be used for extra security, such as validating Product Code at product start. API calls to an AMIs Product Code will not be possible until the product has been published into a limited state for testing.

These Product Codes automatically propagate as customers work with the software. For example, a customer subscribes and launches an AMI, configures it and produces a new AMI. The new AMI will still contain the original Product Code so correct billing and permissions will still be in place. More information is available at Amazon Elastic Compute Cloud (Amazon EC2) instance metadata and user data.

Multiple Versions

AWS Marketplace product listings allow for multiple versions of the product to be available to subscribers as part of their subscription as separate AMIs. The seller can request any number of versions to be available on a product listing. Note that once a subscriber has access to an AMI, they will always have launch permissions on the AMI regardless of the visibility or status of that version on the listing.

For example, product "Data Cleaner" might have versions "1.0.0", "1.2.5" and "2.0.1", all of which can be available to subscribers. If you request removal of version 1.0.0, no new customers can subscribe to that version, but exisiting customer can still access version 1.0.0.

Removing Products from AWS Marketplace

Once your product is published, you can sunset (remove) the product from AWS Marketplace. To remove a product, you identify the product, and submit a request to remove, along with a reason for removeing and a contact email for you. You can also provide a replacement product ID if you are replacing your current product with a new one. Once you request to remove your product, new customers will no longer be able to subscribe. You are required to support any existing customers for a minimum of 90 days. Requests for a product to be removed from AWS Marketplace will be processed with the following conditions:

- The product is removed from AWS Marketplace search, browse and other discovery tools. Any "Subscribe" button or functionality is disabled, and messaging on the page clearly indicates the product is no longer available. Note that the product detail page is still accessible using the URL and may be indexed in public search engines.
- A reason for takedown must be specified (i.e. end of support, end of product updates, replacement product). The Terms and Conditions for AWS Marketplace Sellers contains the requirements for continuing support for these removed products.
- Current subscribers will be messaged by AWS Marketplace informing of the product takedown, reasons, and provide seller contact information.
- Current subscribed customers WILL retain access to the software until they cancel their subscription and will not be impacted in any way.

To remove a product created using the Self-Service Listing tool:

1. Open the AWS Marketplace management portal (AMMP) and choose the **Listings** tab.

2. On your products listing page under current listings, locate the product you want to remove. Under the **Actions** column for the listing, in the **Select action** menu, choose **Remove listing**. An **Remove Product Listing** page will appear.

3. On the **Remove Product Listing** page, next to **Request Reason**, type the reason you are requesting the product be removeed.

4. Next to **Contact Email**, provide the email AWS Marketplace can use to contact you if there are any questions. **Note**: You can also provide a replacement product ID, but the field is not a required field you must complete.

5. Review the information for accuracy, and then choose **Submit Sunset Request**.

Once you have submitted the request, you will be taken to a **What's next** informational page. The AWS Marketplace Seller Operations team will review and process your request. You can check the status of your submission by viewing **Open Requests** from your **Self Service Listing** page. If you have any questions or concerns, contact the **AWS Marketplace Seller Operations** (aws-marketplace-seller-ops@amazon.com) team.

After your product is removed, the product will show in your **Request History** list, and in the **Current Listings** list. In **Current Listings**, the only action available to you will be to download the spreadsheet for the listing. You will no longer be able to edit or submit another sunset request.

For listings not created with the Self-Service Listings tool, you edit and upload the Product Load Form for the product. Links to upload updated Product Load Forms are under the File Uploads tab. For questions on this process, contact the **AWS Marketplace Seller Operations** (aws-marketplace-seller-ops@amazon.com) team.

Best Practices for Building Your AMIs

All AMIs built and submitted to AWS Marketplace must adhere to all product policies. To share your AMI and verify that it meets all AWS Marketplace, utilize the self-service AMI scanning tool. Additionally, here are some best practices and references to help you in building your AMI.

Rights

You are responsible for securing resell rights for non-free Linux distributions, with the exception of AWS-provided Amazon Linux, RHEL, SUSE and Windows AMIs.

Building an AMI

- Ensure your AMI meets all AWS Marketplace policies, including disabling root login.
- Create your AMI in us-east-1 (N. Virginia).
- Products should be created from existing, well-maintained EBS-backed AMIs with a clearly defined life-cycle provided by trusted, reputable sources such as AWS Marketplace.
- Build AMIs using the most up-to-date operating systems, packages, and software.
- All AMIs must start with a public AMI that uses Hardware Virtual Machine (HVM) virtualization and 64-bit architecture.
- Develop a repeatable process for building, updating, and republishing AMIs.
- Use a consistent OS username across all versions and products. We recommend **ec2-user**
- Configure a running instance from your final AMI to the end-user experience you want, and test all installation, features, and performance **prior** to submission to AWS Marketplace.
- Ensure for **Linux** based AMIs that a valid SSH port is open (default is 22) and for **Windows** based AMIs that an RDP port is open (default is **3389**). WINRM (port 5985) must be open to 10.0.0.0/16.

Resources

Creating Your Own AMIs

Creating your Own Windows-based AMIs

Using Amazon EBS-Backed AMIs and Instances

Creating an AMI from an EBS-backed Windows Instance

Amazon Linux

Linux Forums

EC2 Instance Types and Instance Families and Types

Securing an AMI

- Architect your AMI to deploy as a minimum installation to reduce the attack surface. You should disable or remove unnecessary services and programs.
- Whenever possible, use end-to-end encryption for network traffic. For example, use Secure Socket Layer (SSL) to secure HTTP sessions between you and your customers. Ensure that your service uses only valid and up-to-date certificates.
- Use security groups to control inbound traffic access to your instance. Ensure that your security groups are configured to allow access only to the minimum set of ports required to provide necessary functionality for your services. In addition, allow administrative access only to the minimum set of ports and source IP address ranges necessary.
- Consider performing a penetration test against your AWS computing environment at regular intervals; or, consider employing a third party to conduct such tests on your behalf. To learn more, see AWS Penetration Testing (includes a penetration testing request form).
- Be aware of the top 10 vulnerabilities for web applications and build your applications accordingly. To learn more, visit Open Web Application Security Project (OWASP) - Top 10 Web Application Security Risks. When new Internet vulnerabilities are discovered, promptly update any web applications that ship in your AMI. Examples of resources that include this information are SecurityFocus and the NIST National Vulnerability Database.,

Resources

- AWS Security Center
- AWS Security Best Practices
- AWS Overview of Security Processes
- The Center for Internet Security (CIS): Security Benchmarks
- The Open Web Application Security Project (OWASP): Secure Coding Practices Quick Reference Guide
- OWASP Top 10 Web Application Security Risks
- SANS (SysAdmin, Audit, Networking, and Security) Common Weakness Enumeration (CWE) Top 25 Most Dangerous Software Errors
- Security Focus
- NIST National Vulnerability Database

Product and AMI Policies

These policies exist to ensure that the products and offerings on AWS Marketplace contribute to a safe, secure and trusted source for customers.

All products and metadata will be reviewed to ensure they meet or exceed current AWS Marketplace policies. Product policies are always being reviewed and adjusted to meet current security guidelines and it is possible for products to no longer be compliant with current policy. With the introduction of AMI Self Service Scanning, please utilize the self-service AMI scanning tool which will help to ensure the AMI meets AWS Marketplace policies.

Security

1. AMIs **MUST NOT** contain any known vulnerabilities, malware or viruses.

2. AMIs **MUST NOT** contain default passwords, auth keys, key pairs, security keys or other credentials for any reason. All instance authentication must use key pair access rather than password based auth, even if the password is generated, reset or defined by the user at launch.

3. AMIs **MUST NOT** request or use access /secret keys from users to access AWS resources.

4. AWS Marketplace AMIs must not allow password authentication. Disable password authentication via your sshd_config file by setting the PasswordAuthentication to NO.

Accessibility

1. Linux-based AMIs **MUST** lock/disable root login and allow only sudo access through a user account (not "root"). Sudo allows you to control which users are allowed to perform root functions and logs the activity so that there is an audit trail.

2. AMIs **MUST** allow OS-level administration capabilities to allow for compliance requirements, vulnerability updates and log file access. For Linux-based AMIs this is through SSH, and for Windows-based AMIs this is normally through RDP.

3. Linux-based AMIs **MUST NOT** have blank or null root passwords.

4. AMIs **MUST NOT** contain Authorized Passwords or Authorized Keys

5. AMIs **MUST NOT** use default passwords for user interface access. It is recommended to use a randomization process such as using the instance_id from the AWS EC2 Metadata Service.

6. Windows-based AMIs **MUST**

7. Use the most recent version of Ec2ConfigService

8. ENABLE "Ec2SetPassword", "Ec2WindowsActivate" and "Ec2HandleUserData"

9. Remove Guest Accounts or Remote Desktop Users (none are allowed)

10. The seller **MUST NOT** maintain access to the customer's running instances. The customer has to explicitly enable any outside access, and any accessibility built into the AMI must be off by default.

Customer Information

1. All non-BYOL AMI products **MUST NOT** require customer registration with the seller, or require customer information to use the product (for example email address required).

2. Software **MUST NOT** require, collect or export customer data without the customer's knowledge and express consent.

3. AWS **WILL NOT** share private or personally identifying customer information (name, email, contact info, etc.) with any seller or outside party without the consent of the customer.

Product Usage

1. Products **MUST NOT** restrict access to the product or product functionality by time or other restrictions; "Trial", "Beta", or "Evaluation" products are not supported.

2. All AMIs **MUST** meet be compatible with either the AWS 1-click fulfillment experience or the Clusters and AWS Resources feature. For 1-click, the AMI cannot require customer or user data at instance creation in order to function correctly. To learn more about multi-instance or AWS CloudFormation launches see the additional guidelines here.

3. Each AMI **MUST** contain everything a subscriber needs to use the software, including any client applications.

4. For Free or Paid products, the fulfillment process **MUST NOT** require the customer to leave the AWS Marketplace.

5. AMIs **MUST NOT** require a subscription API or launches from outside the AWS Marketplace.

6. Products **MUST NOT** use copyrighted material you do not have the rights to use.

7. Product software and metadata **MUST NOT** contain language that redirects users to other cloud platforms, additional products or upsell services not available on AWS Marketplace.

Architecture

1. Source AMIs for AWS Marketplace **MUST** be provided in the us-east-1 region.

2. AMIs **MUST** use Hardware Virtual Machine (HVM) virtualization

3. AMIs **MUST** use 64-bit architecture

4. AMIs **MUST** be EBS-backed AMIs; we do not currently support S3-backed AMIs.

5. AMIs **MUST** use a supported file system; Ext2, Ext3, Ext4, Xfs, Vfat, Lvm, and NTFS. Encrypted file systems are not supported. These are necessary in order to pass AMI Self Service Scanning.

6. FreeBSD products **MUST** be built from Linux-based OS.

7. AMIs **MUST** be built such that they can run in all regions and is region agnostic. AMIs built differently for regions are not allowed.

AMI File Upload

Self-service AMI scanning is available within the AWS Marketplace Management Portal. With this feature, you can initiate scans of your AMIs and receive scanning results quickly – typically in less than an hour – with clear feedback in a single location. See AMI Self Service Scanning for information on this process.

To upload a new product load form, click on the File Upload tab at the top of the management portal.

From there you will be able to download the most recent product load template. We STRONGLY RECCOMEND checking that the form you have is the most recent as it will be consistently updated with more instance types and regions as they become available. This will significantly increase the ease of loading the page.

AWS Marketplace Listing Checklist

Product Usage

- Production-ready
- Does not restrict product usage by time or any other measurements
- Compatible with 1-click fulfillment experience

- Everything required to utilize the product is contained within the software including client applications
- Default user utilizes a randomized password and/or creation of initial user requires verification that the subscriber is authorized to use the instance using a value unique to the instance such as instance ID

For Free or Paid products:

- No additional license is required to use the product
- Subscriber does not have to provide personally identifiable information (e.g. email address) to use the product **AMI Preparation**
- Utilizes hardware virtual machine (HVM) virtualization and 64-bit architecture
- Does not contain any known vulnerabilities, malware or viruses
- Subscribers have OS-level administration access to the AMI
- Run your AMI through AMI Self Service Scanning

For Windows AMIs:

- Utilizes the most recent version of Ec2ConfigService
- Ec2SetPassword, Ec2WindowsActiviate and Ec2HandleUserData are enabled
- No Guest Accounts or Remote Desktop Users are present

For Linux AMIs:

- Root login is locked/disabled
- No authorized keys, default passwords or other credentials are included

Load Form or Self-service Listings Preparation

- All required fields are completed
- All values are within specified character limits
- All URLs load without error
- Product image is at least 110px wide and between a 1:1 and 2:1 ratio
- Pricing is specified for all enabled instance types (for hourly, hourly_monthly and hourly_annual pricing models)
- Monthly pricing is specified (for hourly_monthly and monthly pricing models)

Software-as-a-Service-Based Products

As a software as a service (SaaS) seller, you deploy software hosted on AWS infrastructure and are responsible for granting AWS Marketplace customers access to the software. There are no AMIs to configure and your customers do not have to run your software on their own EC2 instances. With SaaS, customers subscribe to products through AWS Marketplace, but access the product in your environment. AWS Marketplace offers 2 different pricing models for SaaS listings:

- SaaS Subscriptions
- SaaS Contracts

With **SaaS Subscriptions**, you use the AWS Marketplace Metering Service to report metering usage to AWS. The usage data is used to bill customers for SaaS application use. All charges must be measured and reported every hour from the software deployed in the customer's account.

With **SaaS Contracts**, you use the AWS Marketplace Contract Service to bill customers in advance for the use of your software. Customers pay upfront for a time-bound entitlement to use your SaaS software. Under SaaS Contracts, the customer is entitled to a specified quantity and duration of use of the SaaS product.

With SaaS Subscriptions and SaaS Contracts, customers subscribe to your SaaS listings through AWS Marketplace. After a customer finds and subscribes to your SaaS product on AWS Marketplace, AWS Marketplace passes a billing identifier to your website. Customer account creation, resource provisioning and account management is done through your website or APIs, but access the product in your AWS environment, or through a VPC endpoint service connection you create.

For both SaaS Subscriptions and SaaS Contracts listings, you can use AWS PrivateLink technology, to configure your service as an Amazon Virtual Private Cloud (VPC) endpoint service and your customers can create a VPC endpoint and access your software across the Amazon network. Alternatively, you can provide access to your software product through your website, with customers creating a connection across the Internet.

There are two additional guides available for SaaS products:

- AWS Marketplace SaaS Seller Integration Guide
- AWS Marketplace SaaS Quick Start

Requirements for SaaS Subscriptions and SaaS Contracts listings

SaaS Subscriptions and SaaS Contracts Comparison

As a SaaS application owner offering through AWS Marketplace, you must pick one of two options available for listing and billing your software:

- SaaS Subscriptions (also known as: pay as you go, consumption monetization model)
- SaaS Contracts (also known as: entitlement monetization model)

With SaaS Subscriptions, you use the AWS Marketplace Metering Service to report metering usage to AWS which will be used to bill customers for SaaS application use.

AWS Marketplace Metering Service provides a *consumption* monetization model in which customers are charged only for the number of resources they use in your application. The consumption model is similar to that for most AWS services. Customers pay as they go.

With SaaS Contracts model, you use the AWS Marketplace Contract Service to bill customers in advance for the use of your software. AWS Marketplace Contract Service provides an *entitlement* monetization model in which customers are invoiced in advance for a certain amount of usage of your software, and AWS communicates this *entitlement* to your application. For example, you might sell your customer a certain amount of storage per month for a year, or a certain amount of end-user licenses for 2 years. The customer makes a payment as part of their standard billing cycle.

Table 1: Comparision chart for SaaS Subscription and SaaS Contract models.

	SaaS Subscriptions	SaaS Contracts
Also called	Metering, pay-as-you-go, consumption-based monetization	provisioning-based monetization
How customers use the application	Similar to using an AWS service. Customers subscribe to the listing, get provisioned in seller's environment, and are charged based on usage.	Similar to a classic SaaS application. Customers sign up for capacity up front, and then use the application within the limits of that capacity and duration.
Time granularity of usage	Hourly	1-, 12-, 24-, 36-months options
How sellers communicate with AWS	Sellers send AWS metering records: "Customer X used Y for Z hour"	AWS stores duration, dimension and # of units purchased in dimension, payment, and access details and provides entitlement records to sellers: "Customer X is allowed to use Y dimension until Z date"
When customers are charged	Monthly, within the normal AWS billing cycle.	When the customer purchases an initial contract, upgrades to using more capacity or their capacity is auto-renewed.
Traditional way to realize discounts	Tiered usage plans; pay less per unit for increased usage.	Discounts are incorporated into prices for longer-term commitments or bundles of higher quantities.
Example application	https://aws.amazon.com/marketplace/pp/B074CQY6KB https://aws.amazon.com/marketplace/pp/B075MWZVBM https://aws.amazon.com/marketplace/pp/B0722D4QRN	https://aws.amazon.com/marketplace/pp/B075CRJXNK https://aws.amazon.com/marketplace/pp/B06XXM7JJT https://aws.amazon.com/marketplace/pp/B076J22YD8

SaaS Subscriptions Pricing

For SaaS Subscriptions, AWS Marketplace will bill your customers based on the metering records received by us. Products utilizing SaaS Subscriptions must qualify under one of our seven pricing categories: Users, Hosts, Data, Bandwidth, Requests, Tiers and Units. You will then select the unit of measure for the category selected. You define at least one dimension to offer up to 24 variants for the single listing. All charges must be measured and reported every hour from the software deployed in the customer's account. All usage is then calculated and billed monthly using the same mechanism as AMI based AWS Marketplace offerings. **AWS' ability to bill customers for usage of your product is dependent upon receiving metering records from you. You are responsible for ensuring that your product's metering records are successfully transmitted and received.**

SaaS Contracts Pricing

Products utilizing SaaS Subscriptions must qualify under one of our *five* six pricing categories: Users, Hosts, Data, Bandwidth, Requests, and Units. You will then select the unit of measure for the category selected. You define at least one dimension to offer up to 24 variants for the single listing, as well as the lenth options of the contract. Under the agreement, the customer is entitled to a specified quantity of use of your SaaS product. AWS Marketplace communicates these entitlements to your SaaS application through the AWS Marketplace Entitlement Service. When using SaaS Contracts, your application never sends metering records. Instead, it verifies entitlement by calling the AWS Marketplace Entitlement Service. You are responsible for calling the AWS Marketplace Entitlement Service to determine if a customer is operating within their paid entitlement.

Modeling Contracts Pricing

- Pick a category – Only 1 category per product.
- Units is intentionally ambiguous and can act as a catch-all if the ISV does not bill by any other category available.
- Determine dimensions per product (up to 24 supported).
- Ex: Category = Users. Dimensions = admin, power, read-only, etc.
- Determine contract duration option for the product. Has to be the same across all dimensions.
- Month, 1 year, 2 year, 3 year available. Can pick any combination.
- Determine per unit pricing per dimension for the lowest contract duration term (monthly).
- Ex: Admin user = $4/month, Power User = $3/month, Read Only = $1/month.
- If offering longer terms, multiply the monthly price by 12, 24, or 36.
- For Sellers who would like to offer a tier/package pricing, we also support radio buttons. This means the customer can only purchase one tier, instead of multiple. For example, a customer would select 1 tier of up to 100 GB, and pay a set amount for this contract.
- We do not support validation rules when buying a contract: no minimum, maximum.
- At this time AWS Marketplace does not support charging overage fees, where the Seller can send metering records for units that a customer goes over their contract.

SaaS Subscriptions

**Subscription Flow **

With SaaS Subscriptions and SaaS Contracts, customers subscribe to products through AWS Marketplace, but access the product in the seller's environment. When a customer subscribes to a product, AWS Marketplace passes a billing identifier to the seller. All of the remaining steps (customer account creation, resource provisioning, and account management) occur on the seller's website or with the seller's APIs.

Figure : AWS SaaS billing customer flow.

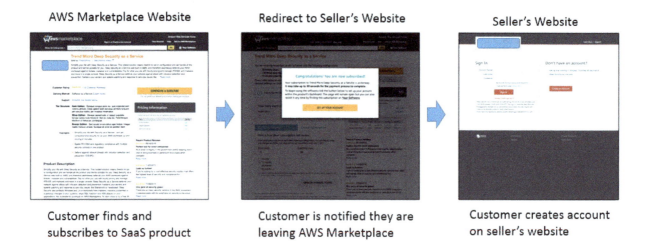

AWS Marketplace Website	Redirect to Seller's Website	Seller's Website
Customer finds and subscribes to SaaS product	Customer is notified they are leaving AWS Marketplace	Customer creates account on seller's website

Metering

Your application will report usage information to AWS, and customers will pay for their use of your SaaS application through their AWS bill based on the metering records you provide. This is an extension of the AWS Marketplace Metering Service (MMS). When your application **meters usage** for a customer, your application is providing AWS with a quantity of usage accrued for a given hour. Your application meters for real units of value, such as gigabytes transferred or hosts scanned in a given hour. AWS uses this information to calculate a customer's bill based on rates that you provide when you create a SaaS listing. Collected transaction proceeds are disbursed to you as an AWS Marketplace seller. It is your responsibility to confirm that your metering is being delivered to AWS Marketplace in a manner that permits AWS to correctly bill your customers for use of your product.

Customer Experience

Under subscribe to products directly on the AWS Marketplace website based on the consumption price displayed on the detail page and recorded in the end user licensing agreement. After subscribing to the product, the customer is directed to the seller's website to register their account and configure the product.

Registering an Account in the SaaS Application

After the customer has subscribed in AWS Marketplace, the customer will register an account in your SaaS application on a website that you host. The registration landing page accepts a token from AWS Marketplace with the customer's identifier for billing.

Using the SaaS Application

Customers access your SaaS application directly through your website or portal using credentials you manage and provide. Customers can find all of the products for which they have active subscriptions under **Your Marketplace Software** in AWS Marketplace when they are signed in to their account. This page contains a link to the page that customers use to sign in to your SaaS application.

Capturing the Amount of Usage

You record and calculate the usage of your software product. As a customer's usage increases or decreases, you send a metering record to AWS Marketplace. These changes can be triggered automatically (by observed customer usage) or manually (as the customer selects a different setting in your application). For example, if you charge based on the amount of data sent into your application, you can measure the amount of data and send a corresponding metering record once an hour. Or you might choose to have customers select a tier of data usage. In this case, you can send a metering record that corresponds to the customer's selection. You can use AWS CloudTrail to verify the record(s) you sent are accurate, and can also use the information to perform audits over time. For more information about the CloudTrail feature, see **Verify Records Using AWS CloudTrail**.

Cancellations

Subscription cancellation must occur through the **Your Marketplace Software** page on the AWS Marketplace website. You will receive notification when a customer cancels a subscription, and you will have one hour to send a final metering record for the customer. You should send a notification from your application that is the cancellation is in progress. If a customer deletes the account or cancels through your application, direct the customer to AWS Marketplace. To guarantee there will be no future charges, customers should confirm cancellation with AWS Marketplace.

Modeling and Listing Your SaaS Product

Before you can list your product on the AWS Marketplace, you need to decide how the product will be priced. Categories and dimensions are used to define your pricing model.

Modeling Your Prices

When pricing your software for SaaS Subscriptions or SaaS Contracts listing, you must first decide on *dimension* category, unit, and dimension(s) and how it will be consumed.

What is a Category?

Category - The type of unit on which customers will be billed. For example, Users, Hosts, Data, or Bandwidth. The category determines how products will be sorted on the AWS Marketplace search page.

What is a Unit?

- **Unit** - The unit of measurement by which customers will be charged for paid products. Options will appear in the drop-down list based on the category you selected. The unit determines how the customer's bill will be presented, and is shown on the pricing box on your product's detail page.

Categories and Units

Currently, AWS supports seven categories for SaaS Subscription and six catagoried for SaaS Contracts.

Seller must pick one category and one matching unit before listing the product through AWS Marketplace. The category and unit cannot be changed once the listing goes public.

Table 1: Categories and Units available for **SaaS Subscriptions** listing.

Category	Valid Unit
[See the AWS documentation website for more details]	[See the AWS documentation website for more details]
[See the AWS documentation website for more details]	[See the AWS documentation website for more details]
[See the AWS documentation website for more details]	[See the AWS documentation website for more details]
[See the AWS documentation website for more details]	[See the AWS documentation website for more details]
[See the AWS documentation website for more details]	[See the AWS documentation website for more details]

Category	Valid Unit
[See the AWS documentation website for more details]	[See the AWS documentation website for more details]
[See the AWS documentation website for more details]	[See the AWS documentation website for more details]

Table 2: Categories and Units available for **SaaS Contracts** listing.

Category	Valid Unit
[See the AWS documentation website for more details]	[See the AWS documentation website for more details]
[See the AWS documentation website for more details]	[See the AWS documentation website for more details]
[See the AWS documentation website for more details]	[See the AWS documentation website for more details]
[See the AWS documentation website for more details]	[See the AWS documentation website for more details]
[See the AWS documentation website for more details]	[See the AWS documentation website for more details]
[See the AWS documentation website for more details]	[See the AWS documentation website for more details]

- **Users** – One AWS customer can represent an organization with many internal users. Your SaaS application can meter for the number of users signed in or provisioned at a given hour. This category is appropriate for software in which a customer's users connect to the software directly (for example, with customer-relationship management or business intelligence reporting).
- **Hosts** – Any server, node, instance, endpoint, or other part of a computing system. This category is appropriate for software that monitors or scans many customer-owned instances (for example, with performance or security monitoring). Your application can meter for the number of hosts scanned or provisioned in a given hour.
- **Data** – Storage or information, measured in MB, GB, or TB. This category is appropriate for software that manages stored data or processes data in batches. Your application can meter for the amount of data processed in a given hour or how much data is stored in a given hour.
- **Bandwidth** – Your application can bill customers for an allocation of bandwidth that your application provides, measured in Mbps or Gbps. This category is appropriate for content distribution or network interfaces. Your application can meter for the amount of bandwidth provisioned for a given hour or the highest amount of bandwidth consumed in a given hour.
- **Request** – Your application can bill customers for the number of requests they make. This category is appropriate for query-based or API-based solutions. Your application can meter for the number of requests made in a given hour.
- **Tiers** – Your application can bill customers for a bundle of features or for providing a suite of dimensions below a certain threshold. This is sometimes referred to as a feature pack. For example, you can bundle multiple features into a single tier of service, such as up to 30 days of data retention, 100 GB of storage, and 50 users. Any usage below this threshold is assigned a lower price as the **standard tier**. Any usage above this threshold is charged a higher price as the **professional tier**. Tier is always represented as an amount of time within the tier. This category is appropriate for products with multiple dimensions or support components. Your application should meter for the current quantity of usage in the given tier. This could be a single metering record (1) for the currently selected tier or feature pack.
- **Units** – Whereas each of the above is designed to be specific, the dimension of Unit is intended to be generic to permit greater flexibility in how you price your software. For example, an IoT product which integrates with device sensors can interpret dimension "Units" as "sensors". Your application can also use units to make multiple dimensions available in a single product. For example, you could price by data and

by hosts using Units as your dimension.

Examples

Pricing Information

This software is priced along a consumption dimension.
Your bill will be determined by the number of hosts you use per hour.

Trend Micro Deep Security as a Service

Hosts	Cost
Any Micro, Small or Medium EC2 instance types	$0.01 / host / hour
Any Large EC2 instance types	$0.03 / host / hour
Any Xlarge or larger EC2 instance types	$0.06 / host / hour
Other Cloud - 1 Core	$0.01 / host / hour
Other Cloud - 2 Cores	$0.03 / host / hour
Other Cloud - 4+ Cores	$0.06 / host / hour
Data Center / Not Cloud	$0.06 / host / hour
Amazon WorkSpaces	$0.01 / host / hour

Pricing Information

This software is priced along a consumption dimension.
Your bill will be determined by the number of units you use.

Elastic Cloud

Units	Cost
US-Small (GB RAM per Hour)	$0.077 / unit
US-Medium (GB RAM per Hour)	$0.041 / unit
US-Large (GB RAM per Hour)	$0.033 / unit
EU-Small (GB RAM per Hour)	$0.107 / unit
EU-Medium (GB RAM per Hour)	$0.057 / unit
EU-Large (GB RAM per Hour)	$0.046 / unit
AP-Small (GB RAM per Hour)	$0.112 / unit
AP-Medium (GB RAM per Hour)	$0.06 / unit

Dimensions

What is a Dimension?

Dimension - Specific aspects of your product that you will bill for. These may be individual tiers, types of hosts scanned, etc. Each of these dimensions will be listed in the pricing box, and can either be metered for using AWS Marketplace Metering Service, or read from AWS Marketplace Entitlement Service, depending on which pricing strategy you've chosen.

With dimensions, any SaaS product must specify either a single dimension or define up to 24 dimensions, each with their own price.

- **Single Dimension** - This is the simplest pricing option. Customers pay a single price per resource unit per hour, regardless of size or volume (for example, $0.014 per user per hour, or $0.070 per host per hour).
- **Multiple Dimensions** – Use this pricing option for resources that vary by size or capacity. For example, for host monitoring, a different price could be set depending on the size of the host. Or, for user-based

pricing, a different price could be set based on the type of user (admin, power user, and read-only user). If you are using tier-based pricing, you should use one dimension for each tier.

Host Scanning Example

Your application analyzes computing hardware for known security vulnerabilities. Customers manually initiate or schedule these scans of their Amazon Elastic Compute Cloud (EC2) instances. As your application performs these scans, it tallies the number of unique hosts scanned every hour. Your application uses the Hosts category. You can declare multiple dimensions for the types of hosts scanned. For example, you can charge different prices for small, medium, and large hosts. Or, if your application is agnostic to the type of hardware scanned, you would use a single dimension.

Log Analysis Example

Your SaaS application digests logs generated by customer applications, reporting trends, and anomalies. As customers upload logs to your application, you measure the quantity of data received in megabytes, gigabytes, or terabytes. Every hour, your application meters for the data uploaded during that hour. Your application uses the Data category. Your application can also meter for the amount of log data stored for any given hour. In this case, your application can meter along two dimensions: data received in the hour and total data stored in the hour. You can continue to meter for data stored until the customer deletes this data or it expires.

Listing Your Product in AWS Marketplace

As an AWS Marketplace seller you can list your products in AWS Marketplace. To list a SaaS product in AWS Marketplace, log into the AWS Marketplace Management Portal and navigate to the **Listings** tab. To create a new SaaS listing, in the **Create a New Product** menu, choose either **SaaS Subscriptions** or **SaaS Contracts**. You must provide:

For SaaS Subscriptions:

- Software by, product title, product description, product logo, EULA, highlights, product category, search keywords, resources, support, refund policy
- The SaaS URL on your details page you want users redirected to (registration landing page owned by the seller that will be used for accepting new customers coming from AWS Marketplace)
- Category and unit of measurement
- Dimension API name, dimension description, dimension rate
- **Accounts to Whitelist** - The account ID(s) you will use for testing your product integration. If you own multiple AWS Accounts that you would like to whitelist to preview this listing, please enter any additional AWS Account IDs in the box below, as a comma-separated list. The account that you are using to create this listing request will be whitelisted by default.
- **SaaS URL** - This is the URL that customers will land on when they enter a billing agreement with your application, and then create an account. This guide covers how you configure this website to retrieve customer billing information automatically.

Dimensions for SaaS Subscriptions have the following:

- **Dimension API Name** - The name used when sending metering records by calling MeterUsage API. This name is visible in billing reports, but because the reports are not external-facing, the name does not have to be user-friendly. The name can be no more than 15 characters and can only include alphanumeric and underscore characters. After you set the name, you will not be able to change it.
- **Dimension Description** - The customer-facing statement that describes the dimension for the product. The description (administrators per hour, per Mbps bandwidth provisioned, etc.) can be no more than 70 characters and should be user-friendly. After the product is published, you will not be able to change this description.
- **Dimension Rate** - The software charge per unit per hour for this product. This field supports three decimal places.

Integration Assistance

This section assumes you have access to the AWS CLI, and have the requisite privileges required to carry forward the integration. This document also assumes that you are registered as a seller in AWS Marketplace, and have submitted a SaaS Subscriptions or SaaS Contracts product that has been published to limited.

Before we begin, we'll want to make sure you have a couple things setup.

Note: Information on setting up the AWS CLI, along with credentials, can be found here. If you are new to the AWS Python SDK, there is a quick start guide here.

IAM USER Policy For AWS Marketplace Actions

In order to enable the service account under which the integration is running, we'll need to define a very constrained IAM policy for that user. Attach this to the IAM user or role you'll use for the integration.

NOTE: The first permission is required for all SaaS integrations. The second and third are only needed for subscriptions and contracts, respectively.

For more information about creating IAM users, see the documentation here. For more information about creating and assigning policies, see the documentation here.

This policy grants access to the APIs for the role or IAM user to which the role is attached. For brevity, this document provides code samples that assume the code is running with the permissions of that user or role. For additional information on how to enable role assumption by another account for these API calls, see the documentation here.

Registration

When a customer chooses **Subscribe** on your SaaS listing in the AWS Marketplace, their browser will be redirected to a page designated by you at product listing using HTTPS. This page should look for the 'x-amzn-marketplace-token' in the form data and pass the registration token value to our API to resolve for the unique customer identifier and corresponding product code. These values will be used to interact with the metering and entitlements APIs, so store them with the associated record.

NOTE: The customer identifier is not the customer's AWS account ID, but it is universal between products.

Configuring Your SaaS Application to Accept New Customers

With SaaS Subscriptions and SaaS Contracts, customers will still have independent accounts registered in your application. You must maintain a website that allows new customers to register an account using billing identifiers provided by AWS. During account creation or sign-in, capture the customer billing identifier and store it along with that customer's other account information.

If your SaaS application will use AWS SaaS Billing with the AWS Marketplace Metering Service, you must:

- Create a registration page or modify the existing one to accept a token from AWS Marketplace that contains a customer identifier that can be stored along with the account registration process.
- Create a process to run every hour that will call a RESTful AWS Marketplace service with the usage for all of your AWS Marketplace customers.

Concepts

- **Customer identifier** – This string represents a customer who is subscribed to your product. It's provided to you by AWS when the customer enters a billing agreement through the AWS Marketplace.

- **Registration token** – Your application receives a registration token from the customer's browser when the customer lands on your registration website. Your application will redeem this registration token for a customer identifier. The registration token is an opaque string.
- **Product code** – This is a unique string for your SaaS application provided to you by AWS. Each AWS listing has one unique product code. It is assigned to you during registration. (Example: a290sds6en72spp3ph4q890es is a product code, b53a9230-6767-4735-a3d9-d5c41caa24c4 is a product id)
- **Subscription notification** – An SNS notification in the following JSON format that informs you when a customer subscribes or unsubscribes to your product. AWS will whitelist your seller AWS account to listen to these notifications on an SNS topic.

The subscription notification can have four actions: subscribe-success, subscribe-fail, unsubscribe-pending, and unsubscribe-success.

Registration Process

The following process takes place when customers purchase your application.

In AWS:

1. When a customer visits your product listing page on the AWS Marketplace website, they choose to subscribe to your product by clicking **Agree to Terms and Register**.

2. The customer's AWS account is **subscribed** to your product. This means metering records sent from your application will become part of the customer's AWS bill.

3. A registration token is generated for the customer that will contain the customer's customer identifier to your website.

4. The customer is redirected to your registration page. This page must be able to accept the token with the customer's identifier.

In your application:

1. The customer's browser sends a POST request to your SaaS registration URL. The request contains one POST parameter, "x-amzn-marketplace-token", containing the customer's registration token. From the perspective of your registration website, the customer has submitted a form with this parameter.

2. Your website must call the **ResolveCustomer** operation on AWS Marketplace Metering Service to redeem this token for a customer identifier and a product code.

3. Your website validates the product code matches your SaaS application identity.

4. Your website must keep this customer identifier in the customer's session. It can be stored temporarily on your server, or it can be part of a signed session cookie on the customer's browser.

5. The customer is instructed to either create an account in your application or sign in to an existing account.

6. The customer is now signed in to your website using credentials specific to that SaaS application. In your accounts database, you can have a row for each customer. Your accounts database must have a column for AWS Customer Identifier, which you'll now populate with the customer identifier you obtained in step 4. **Verify that no other accounts in your system share this customer identifier. Otherwise, you might send conflicting metering records.**

7. During your seller registration process, you will be assigned an SNS topic that will notify you when customers subscribe or unsubscribe to your system. **We recommend that you use SQS to capture these messages.** After you receive a subscription notification with "subscribe-success", the customer account is ready for metering. **Records you send before this notification will not be metered.** Your accounts database should have an extra column for subscription state.

8. Subsequent usage on that account will be metered using the customer identifier stored in your database.

Security and Ordering

As a seller, it's your responsibility to trust only customer identifiers that are immediately returned from AWS or those that are signed by your system. We recommend that you resolve the registration token immediately, because it will expire after one hour. After you resolve the registration token, store the customer identifier as a signed attribute on the customer's browser session until the registration is complete.

Disable Customers Who Unsubscribe

A customer can unsubscribe to your Saas Subscription product through the AWS Management Console. When a customer unsubscribes, the following events occur:

1. Your SaaS application is sent an "unsubscribe-pending" notification through the SNS topic for that customer.

2. You will have one hour to meter any remaining usage for the customer.

3. After this hour, you will receive an "unsubscribe-success" notification. At this point, you can no longer send metering records for this customer.

It's up to you to decide how you want to disable functionality in your SaaS application for unsubscribed customers. For example, your application might complete existing work, but prevent the customer from creating new work. You might want to display a message to the customer that their usage has been disabled. Customers can resubscribe to your product through the AWS Marketplace.

Subscription Notifications

Secondly, we'll need to subscribe to the AWS Marketplace SNS topic that was provided to you during product listing. This topic will provide notifications about changes to customers' subscription and entitlement statuses, allowing you to know when to provide and revoke access for specific customers.

Subscribing an SQS Queue to the SNS Topic

As is mentioned in the AWS SaaS Billing Seller Integration Guide, we recommend subscribing an AWS SQS queue to the provided SNS topic. Detailed instructions on creating an SQS queue can be found here; instructions for subscribing that queue to the provided topic can be found here.

Granting Permissions to Access the Queue

When you subscribe the SQS queue to the provided SNS topic, permissions will automatically be added to allow the SNS topic to publish messages to the queue. However, we still need a policy for granting the API user access to the queue. This can be applied to the same user, if the services will run with the same credentials. Create a policy with the following contents, and attach it to your IAM user (or associated role).

Note: The 'Resource' field will be your SQS Queue ARN.

For more information regarding cross-account SNS and SQS subscription, please see Appendix A at the end of this document.

Polling the SQS Queue for Notifications

Finally, you need to define a service that continually polls the queue, looking for messages and handling them accordingly.

Note: As a **SaaS Subscriptions** seller, you need to handle four actions: **'unsbscibe-success', 'subscribe-fail', 'unsubscribe-pending' and 'unsubscribe-success'.** The only message action you need to handle as a **SaaS Contracts** seller is the **'entitlement-updated'** action. All other actions are required by SaaS Subscription integrations only.

Updating SaaS Products

Once your product is listed on AWS Marketplace, you are responsible for keeping the pricing and product information up-to-date. You make changes to your listing from the AWS Marketplace Management Portal. To make changes, from the **Listings** tab, under **Current Listings** submit the updated information.

AWS Marketplace Contract Service

In SaaS Contracts model, customers are invoiced up-front for quantity of usage purchased. From that point forward, they are **entitled** to use those resources. For example, a customer might purchase a quantity of users who can use your application for a one-month time period, or for one-year, two-year, or three-year time periods.

When the customer buys your software, the customer enters an agreement with you. Under the agreement, the customer is entitled to a specified quantity of use of your SaaS product. AWS Marketplace communicates these entitlements to your SaaS application through the new AWS Marketplace Entitlement Service. Under the SaaS Contract model, your application never sends metering records. Instead, it verifies entitlement by calling the AWS Marketplace Entitlement Service.

Customer Experience

Under the SaaS entitlement model, customers purchase quantities of usage directly on the AWS Marketplace website. The buyer will be able to select specific quantities of varying dimensions or pick a dimension that will have a quantity of 1 in it.

Example of regular drop down (selection of specifc quantities for varying domesnions)

◉ US - 5GB/Day   ○ US - 10GB/Day

○ US - 20GB/Day   ○ US - 50GB/Day

○ US - 100GB/Day   ○ EMEA - 5GB/Day

○ EMEA - 10GB/Day   ○ EMEA - 20GB/Day

○ EMEA - 50GB/Day   ○ EMEA - 100GB/Day

○ APAC - 5GB/Day   ○ APAC - 10GB/Day

○ APAC - 20GB/Day   ○ APAC - 50GB/Day

○ APAC - 100GB/Day   ○ ANZ - 5GB/Day

○ ANZ - 10GB/Day   ○ ANZ - 20GB/Day

○ ANZ - 50GB/Day   ○ ANZ - 100GB/Day

Example of duration selection

How long do you want your contract to run?

◉ 1 month
○ 12 months
○ 24 months
○ 36 months

☑ *I want to opt-in for automatic renewal. I understand that at the end of each term my then current contract configuration will be renewed at the then current prices for the software, which may be found in the pricing section of this page.*

For example, a customer might purchase 10 Users and 20 GB of Data or pick one dimension only, for example:

US -5GB/Day. They can purchase units for the duration offered (1-, 12-, 24, 36-moths options). All of these actions occur on the AWS Marketplace website during the subscription process.

Automatic Renewals

When a customer purchases your product through AWS Marketplace using SaaS contracts, they can agree to automatic renewal of these terms. The customer will continue to pay for the entitlements every month, year, two years, or three years. The customer always has the option to modify the renewal settings. The renewal can be canceled, or the contract can be renewed for entirely different quantities or durations.

The customer can disable renewal themselves or request a canellation and refund though AWS Customer Service. The refund policy is the same as for annual AMI products. Refunds can be granted within 48 hours through AWS Customer Service, or prorated after some duration with seller agreement.

Upgrades

Customers can always upgrade a contract for one of a higher value (for example, higher quantities, longer duration, or higher-value entitlements).Customers will be given a prorated credit for their existing contract.

Example: A customer enters a contract for one user for 12 months for $100, paid every 12 months. Six months into the contract, the customer requires additional users. The customer expands the contract to 10 users for 12 months. The new value is $1,000. After $50 of credit is applied, the customer pays $950. Customers are charged immediately after they make the change to the contract.

Registering an Account in the SaaS Application

After the customer has purchased your product using the entitlement feature, the customer will be directed to the site designated by you to set up an account in your SaaS application. Under this model, the registration landing page for your application works just like the one described in "Configuring Your SaaS Application to Accept New Customers."

Using the SaaS Application

Your SaaS application is agnostic with respect to how your product is purchased or renewed. The customer purchases the product through AWS Marketplace, then provisions or consumes the resources in your SaaS application.

Example: A customer purchased a 1-month contract on April 1st, 2018 for 1 unit priced $100. Ten days into the contract, the customer requires additional units. The customer expands the current contract to 4 units (adding 3 more on April 11th, 2018). The expiration date of contract remains the same: May 1, 2018.

The price for upgrade is calculated on the prorated basis:

Used: 10 days out of 30 days in month of April used 1 unit priced at $100/unit/month = (10/30) x $100 x1 = $33.33

Will use: 20 days remaining to use in a contract for 4 units priced at $100/unit/month = (20/30) x $100 x 4 = $266.66

Since customer already paid $100 when purchased original contract for 1 unit April 1st, 2018, the price to upgrade to 4 units on April 11th, 2018 will be: $200, calculated from ($266.66 + $33.33- $100).

Entitlements are verified by your SaaS application, which makes calls to AWS Marketplace Contract Service, as described in this document.

Modeling and Listing Your SaaS Contracts Product

Under the SaaS Contracts model, the concepts of **categories, units and dimensions** are the same as those in the SaaS Subscriptions pricing model. You must choose a category (Users, Bandwidth, Hosts, Data, Requests, or Units) to represent your application, as well as unit from category selected.

To understand how SaaS Subscriptions (metering, consumption) and SaaS Contracts (entitlements) differ for each category, let's use Data as an example. With SaaS Subscriptions model, your application reports some amount of data processed every hour. With the SaaS Contracts model, a customer might have set aside some amount of storage in your SaaS application. Depending on your choice as seller, the customer might not be allowed to breach this limit. The contract modeled through AWS Marketplace does not include a concept of overage charges. It is up to your SaaS application to prevent usage above the entitled quantity.

Modeling Your Prices for SaaS Contract

After you select a category, unit and one or more dimensions, you must determine the unit costs for each dimension. The unit costs can be for 1-month, 12-months, 24-months, 36-months duration length. You can select to offer one, two, three, or all length options possible for you SaaS Contracts listing. The durations must be the same across each dimension. For example, in a case where you have ReadOnlyUsers and AdminUsers dimensions, if you offer a yearly price for ReadOnlyUsers, you must offer it for AdminUsers, too.

Example: User-based application

You offer an application that allows some number of accounts for a given customer.

	Monthly Price	12-month Price
ReadOnlyUsers	$10/User	$100/User
AdminUsers	$20/User	$200/User

Important: 12-month, 24-month, 36-month price is a one time charge, and NOT a rate charged customer every month. If you offer $10 per unit for 1-month, the price for 12-month option should be $120 or less if you choose to offer a discount, etc.

Example: Data storage application

You offer an application that allows customers to store a certain amount of data in encrypted or unencrypted form. If your application can perform encryption for the customer, you might charge a higher price for this service.

	Monthly Price	12-month Price	24-month Price
Unencrypted Data (GB)	$1.50/GB	$16.00/GB	$30.00/GB
Encrypted Data (GB)	$1.55/GB	$16.60/GB	$31.20/GB

Example: Content distribution

You offer an application that allows customer data to be distributed across several regions. You allow the customer to allocate some dedicated network capacity (bandwidth).

	Monthly Price	12-month Price	24-month Price	36-month Price
Bandwidth (100Mbs)	$100/100Mbs	$1100/100Mbs	$2100/100Mbs	$3000/100Mbs

Listing Your SaaS Contract Product in AWS Marketplace

As an AWS Marketplace seller you can list your products in AWS Marketplace. To list a SaaS product in AWS Marketplace, log into the AWS Marketplace Management Portal and navigate to the **Listings** tab. To create a new SaaS listing, in the **Create a New Product** menu, choose either **SaaS Subscriptions** or **SaaS Contracts**. Required information you must provide includes:

**For SaaS Contracts: **

- Software by, Product title, product description, product logo, EULA, highlights, product category, search keywords, resources, support, refund policy
- The SaaS URL on your details page you want users redirected to (registration landing page owned by the seller that will be used for accepting new customers coming from AWS Marketplace)
- Contract Duration (1-, 12-, 24, 36- months)
- Category and unit of measurement
- Enable Tiered Dimensions option
- Dimension API Name, Dimension Display Name, Dimension Description, Dimension price for durations selected
- Dimension Quantity (optional if you select YES to enable Tiered Dimensions)
- **Accounts to Whitelist**:- The account ID(s) you will use for testing your product integration. If you own multiple AWS Accounts that you would like to whitelist to preview this listing, please enter any additional AWS Account IDs in the box below, as a comma-separated list. The account that you are using to create this listing request will be whitelisted by default.
- **SaaS URL** - This is the URL that customers will land on when they enter a billing agreement with your application, and then create an account. This guide covers how you configure this website to retrieve customer billing information automatically.
- **Enable Tiered Dimensions** – Tiered Dimensions are used for volume tiers or bundles/packages. This also allows you to specify pro-rated pricing with the Dimension Quantity fileds below if desired. Note: It cannot be changed one the listing goes live.
- **Dimension Quantity** – The Quanitity field first compyutes the price per unit for each dimensions, For upgrades to the next tier, it charges for customer additional units based on the per-unit price of the higher tier.
- **Dimension API Name** – The name used when calling Entitlements API. This name is visible in billing reports, but because the reports are not external-facing, the name does not have to be user-friendly. The name can be no more than 15 characters and can only include alphanumeric and underscore characters. After you set the name, you will not be able to change it.
- **Dimension Display Name**: The customer-facing name of a dimension that describes the dimension for the product. The display name which will be visible on AWS Marketplace lsiting to customers (AdminUsers, Silver Tier, Premier Bundle, etc.) can be no more than 24 characters and should be user-friendly. After the product is published, you will be able to change this display name.
- **Dimension Description**: The customer-facing desciption of a dimension that provides additional information about the dimension for the product. The description (Up to 10 Endpoints, 100-250 API calls, etc.) can be no more than 70 characters and should be user-friendly. After the product is published, you will be able to change this description.
- **Dimension - Monthly Price**: The software charge per unit for 1-month option for this dimension. This field supports three decimal places.
- **Dimension - 1 Year Price**: The software charge per unit for 12-month option for this dimension. This field supports three decimal places. It is not a monthly or yearly charge, the price must reflect 12-month one time charge price.
- **Dimension - 2 Years Price:** The software charge per unit for 24-month option for this dimension. This field supports three decimal places. It is not a monthly or yearly charge, the price must reflect 24-month one time charge price.
- **Dimension - 3 Years Price:** The software charge per unit for 36-month option for this dimension. This field supports three decimal places. It is not a monthly or yearly charge, the price must reflect 36-month one time charge price.

Configuring Your SaaS Application to Accept New Customers

Just like SaaS Subscription products that use the consumption model, customers will still have independent accounts registered in your application. You must maintain a website that allows new customers to register an account using billing identifiers provided by AWS. This website can also allow customers to couple an existing account with AWS billing information. During account creation or sign-in, capture the customer billing identifier and store it along with the customer's other account information.

Rather than metering every hour, with SaaS Contracts, your application will periodically verify entitlement (generally, when the customer provisions more resources). The verification can also run periodically, or when the customer visits a dashboard on your SaaS application to provision more capacity. The concepts of **Customer, Registration Token**, and **Product Code** are the same with SaaS Subscriptions (consumption-based) products.

After registering your product, you will have the option to sign up for an SNS topic that will provide notifications about contract creation and modification. Your application should call **GetEntitlements** on AWS Marketplace Entitlement Service to retrieve the customer's entitlement.

Registration Process

The registration process is similar to consumption-based products, with some minor differences.

In AWS:

1. When a customer visits your product listing page on AWS Marketplace, they click **Purchase Users** (or **Purchase Data**, or **Purchase Hosts, etc.**).

2. On the product's fulfillment page, the customer can select quantities of entitlements or select one dimension only with one unit in it (if seller enabled tiers).

3. The customer finalizes the purchase.

4. A registration token is generated that will convey the customer's customer identifier to your website.

5. The customer is redirected to your registration page. This page must be able to accept the token with the customer identifier.

In your application:

1. The customer's browser sends a POST request to your SaaS registration URL. The request contains one POST parameter, x-amzn-marketplace-token, that contains the customer's registration token.

2. Your website must call the **ResolveCustomer** operation on AWS Marketplace Metering Service to redeem this token for a customer identifier and product code.

3. Your website verifies that this product code matches your SaaS application.

4. Your website must keep this customer identifier in the customer's session. It can be stored temporarily on your server, or it can be part of a signed session cookie on the customer's browser.

5. The customer is instructed to either create a new account in your application, or sign in to an existing account.

6. The customer is now signed in to your SaaS application's website using a set of credentials specific to that application. In your accounts database, you might have a row for each customer. Your accounts database should have a column for AWS Customer Identifier, which you'll now populate with the customer identifier you obtained in step 4. **You should verify that no other accounts in your system share this customer identifier. Otherwise, you might have multiple accounts that share entitlement.** This could lead to customers using more capacity in your system by simply creating multiple accounts.

7. Subsequent usage on that account should be verified against AWS Marketplace Entitlement Service. For example, if the customer provisions 10 users on the account, your SaaS application should check AWS Marketplace Entitlement Service for entitlement to that capacity.

Product Pricing

US dollars (USD) is the only supported currency for pricing.

SaaS Subscriptions Pricing

For SaaS Subscriptions, AWS Marketplace will bill your customers based on the metering records received by us. Products utilizing SaaS Subscriptions must qualify under one of our five pricing categories: units, hosts, data, requests, and users. Similar to Usage pricing, you may also define up to 8 variants for the single dimension. All charges must be measured and reported every hour from the software deployed in the customer's account. All usage is then calculated monthly and billed monthly using the same mechanism as AMI based AWS Marketplace offerings. **AWS' ability to bill customers for usage of your product is dependent upon receiving metering records from you. You are responsible for ensuring that your product's metering records are successfully transmitted and received.** For more information, please refer to the AWS Marketplace SaaS Seller Integration Guide.

SaaS Contracts Pricing

For SaaS Contracts, the customer initiates a purchase of your software and enters into an agreement with you. Under the agreement, the customer is entitled to a specified quantity of use of your SaaS product. AWS Marketplace communicates these entitlements to your SaaS application. This is done through the AWS Marketplace Entitlement Service. When using SaaS Contracts, your application never sends metering records. Instead, it verifies entitlement by calling the AWS Marketplace Entitlement Service. You define the categories, dimensions, and variants, as well as the length of the contract.

AMI Pricing Models

AWS Marketplace has multiple pricing models for AMI products. **NOTE:** Sellers of paid AMI products **must** be able to provide a W-9 tax form (for U.S. based entities) or a W-8 form (for EU- based entities) as described in Section 1.1.1.

Pricing Model	Description
Bring Your Own License (BYOL)	AWS Marketplace does not charge customers for usage of the software, but customers must supply a license key to activate the product. This key is purchased outside of AWS Marketplace. The entitlement/ licensing enforcement, as well as all pricing and billing are handled by the seller.
Free	Customers are allowed to run as many instances as EC2 supports with no additional software charges incurred.

Pricing Model	Description
Hourly	**Hourly:** Software is charged by the hour. Each instance type can be priced differently (but is not required to be) and usage is rounded up to the nearest whole hour. **Hourly with Free Trial:** Customers are allowed to run exactly 1 instance of the software without incurring a charge for a predetermined set of days between 5 and 30 days as decided by the seller. The Free Trial applies to the most expensive instance type that is running, and any concurrent usage outside the 1 instance is billed at the hourly rate. NOTE- this is a different model than the AWS Free Tier for EC2 usage where customers are given a bucket of 750 hours of free usage each month. **Hourly with Monthly:** Both Hourly and Monthly charges are applied independently; the monthly fee is charged every month regardless of usage, the hourly fee is applied based on hourly usage only. **Hourly with Annual:** Customers have the option to purchase a year's worth of usage upfront for one EC2 instance of one instance type. Sellers set the pricing for each instance type and can offer net savings over the hourly price (not required). Any customer usage above the number of annual subscriptions purchased is billed at the hourly rate set by the seller for that instance type. **Hourly with Free Trial and Annual:** This is identical to the Hourly model with an Annual option, except it includes a Free Trial allowing a customer to run 1 instance of any instance type for free for a seller set number of days. Annual subscriptions can be purchased at any time, and they are combined additively with the Free Trial subscription.
Monthly	**Monthly:** Software is paid for on a fixed monthly basis, regardless of number of instances the customer runs. Monthly Charges are pro-rated at sign-up and upon cancellation, e.g.: a customer who subscribes for 1 day of the month will be charged for 1/30th of the month. **Monthly with Hourly:** Both Hourly and Monthly charges are applied independently; the monthly fee is charged every month regardless of usage, the hourly fee is applied based on hourly usage only. **NOTE: Free Trial and Annual pricing cannot be combined with Monthly pricing**

Pricing Model	Description
Usage	**Usage:** Software is directly charged for the value the seller provides along with one of four dimensions: users, data, bandwidth, or hosts. You may define up to 8 variants for the single dimension. All charges are still incurred hourly by the customer. All usage is calculated monthly and billed monthly using the same mechanism as existing AWS Marketplace software. Usage pricing is also referred to as AWS Marketplace Metering Service **NOTE: Free trial and Annual pricing cannot be combined with Usage pricing**

General Pricing Policies

- For Paid Listings, AWS Marketplace collects software charges from the customer.
- There is no service fee for BYOL products listed on AWS Marketplace. However, in order to deliver on our customer promise of selection, we require that all BYOL products also have a paid option so that customers who don't have existing licenses have the option to purchase and use the products. We realize that the online purchase of software is a departure from how some companies do business, so for the first 90 days after launch we will relax the requirement that this software be accompanied by a version available for purchase on AWS Marketplace. During this time, the AWS Marketplace account management teams will work with software sellers to address challenges and to determine if and how the software can be made available for purchase on AWS Marketplace.
- There is no service fee for Free or Open Source Software that is made available to customers without charge.

AWS charges vs Software charges

- All AMI-based products will incur associated AWS infrastructure charges depending on the services and infrastructure used. These rates and fees are defined and controlled by AWS, and can vary between regions. See EC2 Pricing for more information.
- For Paid, the seller defines the charges for using the software.

These 2 types of prices are displayed separately on the AWS Marketplace detail pages to provide customers with a clear understanding of potential cost for using the products. For example:

Free Trial

Hourly products are eligible for the optional "Free Trial" program, where a customer can subscribe to the product and use a single instance for up to 31 days without paying any software charges on the product. Applicable AWS infrastructure charges still apply. Simply define the duration of the trial period (5 to 31 days) and notify the AWS Marketplace team at aws-marketplace-seller-ops@amazon.com.

When a customer subscribers to a Free Trial product they are sent a Welcome email that includes the term of the Free Trial, a calculated expiration date and details on unsubscribing. 3 days prior to the expiration date a reminder email is sent.

If you are offering a Free Trial product in AWS Marketplace, you agree to the specific refund policies for Free Trials, located in Special Guidelines documentation.

Annual Pricing

An Annual pricing model allows you to offer products to customers who can purchase a 12-month subscription. The subscription pricing can provide up to 40% savings versus running the same product hourly for extended periods. The customer is invoiced for the full amount of the contract at the time of subscription. To read more about the benefits of offering an Annual product, please see the Annual Subscriptions FAQ on the AWS Marketplace site.

Some notes and callouts when working with an Annual product in AWS Marketplace:

- Annual pricing is defined per instance type. It can be the same for all EC2 instance types or different for each instance type.
- All Annual instance types must also have an Hourly instance type defined. AWS Marketplace does not offer Annual-only pricing or Hourly without Annual on the same product; for any product offering Annual pricing, Hourly pricing also needs to be specified.

- A \$0 Annual price is allowed on a specific instance type, if the Hourly price is also \$0 and there are other non-\$0 Annual instance types defined.
- At the end of Annual subscription period, the customer will start being charged at the Hourly price.
- If a customer buys X Annual subscriptions but is running Y software on Y instances, then the customer will be charged at Hourly software price for (Y-X) instances which are not covered by Annual subscriptions. As such, an Hourly rate must be included for all Annual pricing instance types.

If you are offering an Annual product in AWS Marketplace, you agree to the specific refund policies for Annual products, located in the File Uploader documents section of AWS Marketplace Management Portal.

Usage Pricing

The AWS Marketplace Metering Service enables you to define additional dimensions you want to charge your customers for the value your software provides. As a seller, you can choose one of the dimensions from the following: Users, Hosts, Bandwidth, or Data. You may also define up to 8 variants for the single dimension. All charges must be measured and reported every hour from the software deployed in the customer's account. All usage is calculated monthly and billed monthly using the same mechanism as existing AWS Marketplace software.

Using the AWS Marketplace Metering Service, you can handle several new pricing scenarios. For instance, if your software monitors hosts, you can charge for each host monitored and set different pricing based on the host size. If your software allows multiple users across an organization, you can charge by user. Each hour, the customer would be charged for the total number of provisioned users.

Note: In the product load form, relevant columns are named as Flexible Consumption Pricing (FCP).

Additional callouts about AWS Marketplace Metering Service products:

- If your software is already listed on AWS Marketplace, you will need to create a new product to enable an alternate usage dimension. That is, currently, we are unable to convert a standard listing to use the AWS Marketplace Metering Service. After the new product is published, you have a choice of taking down the old listing or keep both on site.
- The AWS Marketplace Metering Service requires that your software report usage ever hour, recording the customer usage for the hour. If there is a failure in the transmission or receipt of metering service records, AWS will not be able to bill for such usage. You are responsible for ensuring the successful receipt of metering records.
- At this time, products that use the AWS Marketplace Metering Service do not support 1-Click. Subscribers are required to launch your software with an IAM role with specific permissions and have an Internet Gateway.
- Free Trial and Annual Pricing are not compatible with the AWS Marketplace Metering Service at this time.
- Changing dimension (user, hosts, bandwidth, and data) or dimension name is not supported. You will need to create a new listing.

Private Offers

The AWS Marketplace Seller Private Offer program allows AWS Marketplace sellers to negotiate custom pricing and end user license agreements with individual AWS Marketplace customers (buyers). Once the seller and buyer agree on pricing and EULA terms, the seller can create an offer for a specific buyer. To take advantage of this program you must be part of the AWS Marketplace Enhanced Data Sharing Program.

You create private offers through the AMMP. To create an offer, you select the **Private Offer** tab from the portal landing page. From the **Manage Private Offer** page, you can create a new offer. When you create a new offer, you select a product from a pull-down menu and provide the account number for the customer you are making the offer to. You then set the pricing for your offer and upload a PDF version of the EULA for the offer. After that, you set a time duration (number of days) the offer will be in effect once accepted by the customer, and a date the customer must accept the offer by. If the customer does not accept the offer by the date you set, the offer is no longer available.

Once you have formed your offer, you review (and edit if necessary) the offer. When you are satisfied with your offer, you extend the offer to the intended customer. The offer takes approximately 45 minutes to process, and then will be listed on the Manage Private Offer page. The offer will have a URL to the fulfillment page for the offer that you can copy, and then email to the customer. The customer also can navigate to your product page and there will be a banner on the page indicating a private offer is available.

Once you extend the offer to your customer, you cannot edit or cancel the offer. Instead, if you need to update the terms of an offer you would need to create a new offer.

Refunds

All Paid Listings, regardless of pricing model, must have a stated refund policy for software charges. The policy must include the terms of the refund as well as a method of contacting the seller to request a refund. While the details of the refund policy are up to the seller, we highly encourage you to offer customers some manner of refund for usage of the product. We expect sellers to comply with their posted policies when AWS Marketplace users request refunds.

- Except as noted below* all software refunds must be approved by the seller via the form below, and will be processed and issued upon your direction by AWS.
- *Special cases exist for products using Free Trial, Annual and Usage pricing types where you agree that AWS may initiate and process such refunds without further approval or direction from you. Please see the "Special Guidelines" document, accessible on the AMMP.
- Customers requesting a software refund directly from AWS will be directed to contact the seller.
- Refunds of any AWS infrastructure charges are up to the discretion of AWS and are handled independently of software refunds.
- Monthly subscriptions are pro-rated based on the date the user subscribes and the date they cancel and are processed automatically and require no action on your part.
- For example, if a user signs up on 3/1, they will be charged the full rate for March and the full rate for all subsequent months they are subscribed to the software. If the user signs up on 3/15, they will be charged half the monthly fee for March (and then the full monthly fee for April, May and so on). Pro-rated refunds associated with cancellations will be issued based on the same tenants.

If you use the AWS Marketplace Tax Calculation Service, customers may reach out to you to request a tax-only refund. If a customer requests a tax-only refund, you can, at your discretion, grant either a tax-only refund or a full software refund plus tax.

Refund Process

For a seller to initiate a software refund for a customer:

1. Record the following information from the customer:

2. The customer's email address (associated with his/her AWS account).

3. The customer's AWS Account number. (The account number can be found on the customer's AWS Account Activity screen in the upper right-hand corner).

4. The billing period(s) for which the customer would like a refund.

5. Navigate to the AWS Marketplace seller refund request form.

6. Provide the customer's information in the form.

7. Provide the Product ID for the product you're trying to refund. The Product ID can be found in your daily Subscription Report.

8. For **Annual products** where a customer is requesting a refund, upgrade or downgrade:

9. Verify the customer has purchased an annual subscription using your Subscriber Report (there may be a 24-hour delay).

10. Provide a new Subscription Cancellation Date in the comments field.

11. Provide a description of the change you are authorizing (refund, upgrade, downgrade) in the comments field.

12. Submit the form.

13. AWS will be notified and will process the refund and issue it to the customer. It should show up within 2-3 hours on the customer's AWS account.

14. For **Annual products**, we will also update the end date of the subscription to match that provided in the request form.

Changing Prices

Changes to pricing and metadata can be done through the AMMP. In the portal, under the **Listings** tab, you will find a list of current products that you created through the AMMP. In the table for your current listings there is an Action column that provides an option for you to edit your listing.

Changing Pricing Models

Changes to pricing models must be reviewed and approved by AWS Marketplace to ensure a positive customer experience and reduced risk to all parties. Please discuss what pricing model changes are possible with the AWS Marketplace Seller Operations team at aws-marketplace-seller-ops@amazon.com. All requests for pricing model changes can take 30-90 days to process and review.

Pricing Your Software with SaaS

When pricing your software with the AWS Marketplace Metering Service, you must first decide on a usage category and how it will be consumed. At this time, the service supports six distinct pricing scenarios. You must select only one of these for your product:

- Provisioned user (per hour)
- Concurrent user (per hour)
- Provisioned host (per hour)
- Concurrent host (per hour)
- Provisioned bandwidth (per hour)
- Accumulated data (per hour)

Next, you must decide how to price the selected usage category:

- Single price
- Multiple dimensions (up to eight)

Example: Provisioned Bandwidth with Non-Linear Pricing

Imagine you offer network appliance software. You choose to bill by provisioned bandwidth. For your usage category, select bandwidth. In addition to charging by bandwidth, you want to charge a different price as buyers scale up. You can define multiple dimensions within the bandwidth category. You can define a distinct price for 25 Mbps, 100 Mbps, and 1 Gbps.

Example: Concurrent Hosts with Multiple Dimensions

Imagine you offer software that monitors other Amazon EC2 instances. You choose to bill by the number of hosts that are being monitored. For your usage category, select host. In addition to charging by host, you want to charge for the extra value for monitoring larger hosts. You can use multiple dimensions within the host category. You can define a distinct price for micro, small, medium, large, x-large, 2XL, 4XL, 8XL instances. Your software is responsible for mapping each particular host to one of your defined dimensions. Your software is responsible for sending a separate metering record for each dimension of your usage category if applicable.

Listing Your SaaS Product on AWS Marketplace

To take advantage of the Metering Service, you must create a new product listing. If your software is already listed on the AWS Marketplace, you will need to decide whether the new AWS Marketplace Metering Service product will be made available in addition to your current listing, or if it will replace your current listing as the only version available to new users. If you choose replacement, the existing product will be removed from the AWS Marketplace so that it is no longer available for new subscribers. Existing customers will continue to have access to their old product and instances, but they can migrate to the new product at their convenience. The new product must meter usage to the AWS Marketplace Metering Service.

After you have your AMI, follow the standard process to share and scan your AMI using the self-service tool. In addition, using the template available on the management portal, fill out the product load form and upload it to start the ingestion process.

The following definitions will help you fill out the fields of the product load form for the AWS Marketplace Metering Service. On the product load form, these fields are labeled as Flexible Consumption Pricing (FCP) to differentiate them from hourly and monthly priced products.

- **Title**: If you already have a listing on AWS Marketplace and you are adding the same listing with the AWS Marketplace Metering Service, include the FCP category/dimension in parenthesis to differentiate the two (for example, "PRODUCT TITLE (Data)").
- **Pricing Model**: From the drop-down list, choose **Usage**.
- **FCP Category**: The category in which customers will be charged for paid products with a **Usage** pricing component. From the drop-down list, choose **Users**, **Hosts**, **Data**, or **Bandwidth**.
- **FCP Unit**: The unit of measurement on which customers will be charged for paid products with a **Usage** pricing component. Options will appear in the drop-down list based on the FCP category you selected. The following table lists the valid units for each category.

Category	Valid Units
Users	UserHrs
Hosts	HostHrs
Data	MB, GB, TB
Bandwidth	Mbps, Gbps

- **FCP Dimension Name**: The name used when sending metering records by calling MeterUsage API. It is visible in billing reports, but because it is not external-facing, the name does not need to be user-friendly. The name can be no more than 15 characters and can only include alphanumeric and underscore characters. **After you set the name, you will not be able to change it. Changing the name requires a new AMI.**
- **FCP Dimension Description**: The customer-facing statement that describes the dimension for the product. The description (for example, Administrators per hour, Per Mbps bandwidth provisioned) can be no more than 70 characters and should be user-friendly. **After the product is published, you will not be able to change this description.**
- **FCP Rate**: The software charge per unit for this product. This field supports 3 decimal places.

Notes:

- You do not need to fill out hourly and annual pricing fields.
- Free trial and annual pricing are not compatible.
- Currently, products that use the Clusters and AWS Resources feature cannot use the AWS Marketplace Metering Service.
- Price, instance type, or region change will follow the regular process as other AWS Marketplace products.
- Products with the AWS Marketplace Metering Service cannot be converted to other pricing models such as hourly, monthly, or BYOL.
- We recommend adding IAM policy information in your usage instructions or document.

If you have questions, contact the **AWS Marketplace Seller Operations** (aws-marketplace-seller-ops@amazon.com) team

Modifying Your SaaS Software to Use the Metering Service

You will need to modify your software to record customer usage, send hourly usage reports to the Metering Service, and handle new failure modes. The software operates independently of pricing, but the software will need to know about the usage category, how it is consumed, and any dimensions.

Measuring Consumption

Your software must determine how much of the selected usage category and which dimensions the customer has consumed. This value will be sent, once each hour, to the AWS Marketplace Metering Service. In all cases, it is assumed that your software has the ability to measure, record, and read consumption of resources for the purpose of sending it on an hourly basis to the Metering Service.

For provisioned consumption, this will typically be read from the software configuration as a sampled value, but might also be a maximum configured value, recorded each hour. For concurrent consumption, this might be either a periodic sample or a maximum value recorded each hour. For accumulated consumption, this will be a value that is accumulated each hour.

For pricing on multiple dimensions, multiple values must be measured and sent to the Metering Service, one per dimension. This requires your software to be programmed or configured with the known set of dimensions when providing the AMI for listing. The set of dimensions cannot change after a product is listed.

For each pricing scenario, this table describes recommended ways for measuring consumption each hour:

Scenario	How to Measure
Provisioned User	Current number of provisioned users (sampled). -OR- Maximum number of provisioned users (seen that hour).
Concurrent User	Current number of concurrent users (sampled). -OR- Maximum number of concurrent users (seen that hour). -OR- Total number of distinct users (seen that hour).
Provisioned Host	Current number of provisioned hosts (sampled). -OR- Maximum number of provisioned hosts (seen that hour).
Concurrent Host	Current number of concurrent hosts (sampled). -OR- Maximum number of concurrent hosts (seen that hour). -OR- Total number of distinct hosts (seen that hour).
Provisioned Bandwidth	Current provisioned bandwidth setting (sampled). -OR- Maximum provisioned bandwidth (seen that hour).

Scenario	How to Measure
Accumulated Data	Current GB of data stored (sampled). -OR- Maximum GB of data stored (seen that hour). -OR- Total GB of data added or processed that hour. -OR- Total GB of data processed that hour.

Call AWS Marketplace Metering Service

Your software must call the Metering Service hourly and record the consumption value for that hour.

When your software starts, it should record the minute-of-the-hour at which it started. This will be referred to as the *start-minute*. Every hour on the start-minute, your software must retrieve the consumption value for that hour and call the Metering Service.

To wake up each hour at the start-minute, your software will need to use one of three approaches:

1. A thread within your software.

2. A daemon process that starts up with the instance or software.

3. A cron job that is configured during application startup.

Your software must call the AWS Marketplace Metering Service using the IAM role configured on the customer's instance and specify the consumption dimension and amount.

Your software can use the AWS SDK to call the AWS Marketplace Metering Service. The following is a typical implementation:

1. Use the instance profile to create a service client. This requires the role configured for the EC2 instance. The role credentials are refreshed by the SDK automatically.

AmazonMeteringService meteringClient = new AmazonMeteringService(new InstanceProfileCredentialsProvider());

1. Each hour, read your software configuration and state to determine consumption values for that hour. This might include collecting a value-per-dimension.

2. Call the **meterUsage** method on the SDK client with the following parameters (call additionally for each dimension that has usage):

- **timestamp**: timestamp of the hour being recorded. (Use UTC.)
- **productCode**: product code assigned to the software.
- **dimension**: dimension(s) assigned to the software
- **quantity**: consumption value for the hour

In addition, your software must call an in-region AWS Marketplace Metering Service endpoint. Your product must have a correct regional endpoint setup, so us-east-1 sends records to us-east-1 endpoint, and us-west-2 sends records to us-west-2 endpoint. Making in-region calls provides buyers with a more stable experience and prevents situations in which an unrelated region's availability could impact software running in another region.

and

When you send metering records to the service, you must connect to the AWS Marketplace Metering Service in your region. Use the **getCurrentRegion()** helper method to determine the region in which the EC2 instance is running, and then pass this region information to the MeteringServiceClient constructor. If you do not specify a region in the SDK constructor, it will default to the us-east-1 region. If your application attempts to make cross-region calls to the service, it will be rejected.

Important Information About Failure Handling

Your product must send metering records to the service, a public internet endpoint, so that usage can be captured and billed. **Because it is possible for a customer to modify network settings in a way that prevents your metering records from being delivered, your product should account for this by choosing a failure mode.**

Typically, software can fail open (provide a warning message but maintain full functionality) or fail closed (disable all functionality in the application until a connection has been reestablished). You can choose to fail open, closed, or something specific to your application. **We strongly recommend that you refrain from failing closed after less than two hours of metering failures.**

As an example of failing partially open, you could continue to allow access to the software but not allow the buyer to modify the software settings. Or, a buyer could still access the software, but would not be able to create additional users. **Your software is responsible for defining and enforcing this failure mode.** Your software's failure mode must be included when your AMI is submitted, and it cannot be changed later.

Refund policy

If you list your software as a free trial product, AWS can issue refunds on your behalf for software charges accruing within seven days of a conversion from a free trial to a paid subscription. Refunds issued in connection with free trial conversions require no action on your part. By enabling Free Trial on a product, you are agreeing to this policy.

AWS Marketplace for US IC

Refund Policy

For software listed on the IC Marketplace, AWS can issue a full refund for software charges incurred by end users within 30 days of subscription to the product. Refunds will be decided and executed by the AWS team and require no action on your part. By listing a product in the IC Marketplace, you are agreeing to this policy

Annual Products

These listing guidelines apply to all Sellers who are offering a product on AWS marketplace with annual pricing.

Price Change

You can change annual prices (the $ value, for example $1000/year to $1200/year) whenever desired but with 90 day notice to existing customers of annual pricing. The new price will apply to new subscriptions but will have no impact on existing subscriptions. Price changes will be effective for auto-renewals only if the price was changed at least 90 days before the auto-renewal date. The customer will receive an email prior to auto-renewal that includes the new price.

Refund / Cancellation / Upgrade / Downgrade

For uniform and great customer experience, AWS requires Sellers to implement the following cancellation/change windows:

Applicable policy	Time period / window	Who can authorize it
Full refund cancellation (Cancel with 100% refund)	Within 48 hours of purchase	AWS CS (Customer support) or Seller

Applicable policy	Time period / window	Who can authorize it
Pro-rata refund cancellation (Cancel with pro-rata refund)	Within 14 days of purchase	Seller only
Downgrade subscription (Replace existing subscriptions with less expensive subscription)	Within 30 days of purchase	Seller only
Upgrade subscription (Replace existing subscriptions with more expensive or same priced subscription)	Any time during 12 months	AWS CS (Customer support) or Seller
Full refund cancellation in case of auto-renewal	Within 14 days of purchase	AWS CS (Customer support) or Seller

Please note that:

- You should not include windows length and other details in product details/description
- Upgrade/ downgrade is essentially a 2-step process for customer; buy new subscriptions and request cancellation of old subscription with refund
- In some cases (as noted above), AWS may issue refunds on your behalf. No action on your part is required to process those refunds.

End User License Agreement

AWS customer's usage of software for 12 months under annual subscription is covered by the EULA you have provided on your product's details page on AWS Marketplace.

Refund Policy

If you meter the usage of your software using the AWS Marketplace Metering Service, AWS can issue refunds on your behalf for software charges resulting from software metering errors. If these errors are common across multiple customers, AWS may determine an appropriate refund for each customer and apply it directly to each customer. Refunds issued in connection with the AWS Marketplace Metering Service must be confirmed with the seller once, but does not require the seller to confirm each individual refund. By using the AWS Marketplace Metering Service with a product, you are agreeing to this policy.

Categories and Metadata

Here are best practices, tips and notes on supplying product metadata. AWS Marketplace will make revisions to the product metadata provided solely for quality assurance and error correction.

Naming and Describing Your Product

The information about your product becomes the face of the product to customers. As you decide on your product name, description, highlights, and so on, consider using information that is both compelling and differentiates your software from other software.

The information you provide is important to ensure that potential customers have enough information to make informed acquisition and buying decisions.

Optimizing the Product Name Field

Keep the following guidelines in mind as you create the product name.

- Use title case (first letter of each word is capitalized)
- Ensure that a customer can identify the product by the name alone
- Use the name of the brand or manufacturer
- Do not include descriptive data or hyperbole

Example: Smart Solution Load Balancer - Premium Edition

Writing the Product Description

The product description lists the product's features, benefits, usage, and provides other relevant and specific product information. The description can be up to 350 characters long. A customer might read the description if they are interested enough to learn more about the product than is obvious from the name or highlights.

Keep the following guidelines in mind as you create the product description.

- Avoid unnecessary capitalization
- Avoid unnecessary punctuation marks
- Do not include redirect information
- Check spelling and grammar
- Include only critical, useful information

Example: Smart Solution automatically distributes incoming application traffic across multiple Amazon EC2 instances. It enables you to achieve even greater fault tolerance in your applications, seamlessly providing the amount of load balancing capacity needed in response to incoming application traffic. Smart Solution detects unhealthy instances within a pool and automatically reroutes traffic to healthy instances until the unhealthy instances have been restored. Customers can enable Smart Solution within a single AWS availability zone or across multiple zones to ensure more consistent application performance.

Writing the Product Highlights

The product information page displays up to three product highlight bullet points. The descriptive text you write for each highlight should describe the product's primary selling points in brief, informative, and easy-to-understand language.

Example: Projecting Costs - With Smart Solution, you only pay for what you use. You are charged for each hour or partial hour your Smart Solution is running.

Writing the Release Notes

Each time you update an AMI product, you must provide a description of the changes in release notes. Your release notes should contain specific information to help the user decide whether to install the update. Use clear labels for the update, such as "Critical" for a security update or "Important" or "Optional" for other types of updates.

Writing the Usage Instructions

The usage instructions are critical to ensure that each user is able to successfully configure and run the software. This field will display during the AMI configuration process so the usage instructions must contain all information the user will need. Failure to provide clear instructions could result in unnecessary support contacts.

- Usage instructions should be written with a new or moderately technical person in mind and not necessarily an IT Manager or Engineer. It is also best not to assume the user has prior experience with or extensive knowledge of the product, or computer operating systems.
- Usage should take the customer from 1-click launch all the way to using the product, including any configuration or special steps to get the application running.

Example:

1. Launch the product via 1-click.

2. Access the application via web browser at https://<EC2_Instance_Public_DNS>/index.html.

3. Login using the username "user" and the instance_id of the instance as the password.

Choosing Categories and Keywords

When you list your product, you can choose up to three software categories and corresponding subcategories for your product. This helps customers discover your product as they browse or search the listings on AWS Marketplace. Please choose only categories that are relevant to your product. In most cases, only one category will apply. The **Product Load Form and Self-Service Listings portal both** contain a complete list of categories.

Note: Categories are not the same as keywords. The categories and subcategories available are predefined for AWS Marketplace and you decide which categories and subcategories apply to your product by selecting these from a list during the listing process. Keywords are not predefined, but are created during the listing process. You do not need to add the category as a keyword.

Creating Search Keywords

During the product listing process, you can enter up to three keywords (single words or phrases) to help customers discover your product through site searches. The field for the keywords can contain a **maximum of 50 characters**.

The following tips can help you to create a relevant set of search keywords.

- Use terms that are relevant so that customers can easily find your products
- Choose keywords from your customer's vocabulary—that is, choose words and phrases that customers are likely to use when thinking about your type of product
- Create keywords based on specific features in your product
- The product title is already indexed in our search; the terms you submit should not contain the title of your product

Note: Keywords are not the same as software categories. Keywords are more specific terms that are related to your product.

Submitting Your Listing for Publication

Product submission is the process used to make your products available to AWS Marketplace customers. There are two tools used to submit products for publication in the AWS Marketplace. The Self-service Listing (SSL) tool is a menu-driven tool available on the AWS Marketplace Management Portal (AMMP) you use to submit or edit product offerings. The other tool is the Product Load Form, also available on the AMMP. Use this table to determine whether you can submit your product using the SSL tool or will need to complete and submit the Product Load Form:

**Pricing Model **Yes = product submission using SSL No = product submission using Product Load Form	**Products launched using Single-Node AMI **	Products launched with AWS Cloud-Formation	Products launched as Software as a Service (SaaS)
Bring Your Own License (BYOL)	Yes	No	
Free	Yes	No	
Hourly	Yes	No	
Hourly with Annual	Yes	No	
Monthly	No	No	
Hourly with Monthly	No	No	
Usage (MMS)	No	No	
SaaS Subscription			Yes
SaaS Contract			Yes
SaaS Legacy			No

You can submit products individually, or can submit multiple products at the same time. Bulk submissions (new products or updates to products) cannot be completed using the SSL tool. If you are unclear on what products can be submitted in what manner, we recommend you first try submitting your product using the SSL tool and only use the product load form if you cannot submit your products with SSL. If you have any problems making your submissions, contact the AWS Marketplace Seller Operations team at aws-marketplace-seller-ops@amazon.com.

Self-Service Listings

Self-Service Listings is under the Listings tab of the AMMP. To access Self-Service Listings, log in to the AMMP and navigate to the Listings tab. You can also track the status of your product listing requests, and view your request history. Once you start a new product listing request, you can save your work in progress if necessary and create your listing in several different sessions.

When you are ready to submit your product, your submission will be reviewed by the AWS Marketplace team. You can monitor the status of your request on the Self-Service Listings dashboard. For new products, once your listing has been approved for publication, you will receive a Limited listing URL where you can preview and approve your submission prior to the listing going live. Updates to your existing listings will be published directly to site. This includes adding/removing versions, and metadata changes.

Requests are listed in the SSL dashboard under **Requests**. There are two tabs, **Open Requests** and **Request History**. Your submissions will be listed as an open request until all processing of the request is complete. For each request, the list will have the request date, product title, request type, request status, and action needed. The status will be one of the following:

- **In Draft** – you have started the request process but have not submitted your request.

- **Submitted** – you have completed and submitted your request and it is under review.
- **Action Required** – AWS Marketplace has reviewed your request and needs additional information.
- **Approval Required** – AWS Marketplace has created the limited listing page for your product and you must review and approve or reject the listing page before AWS Marketplace will publish. If you approve, the status changes to **Publishing Pending** while the site gets published. If you reject, the status returns to **In Draft** so you can modify the listing.
- **Publishing Pending** – You have approved the mock-up of your listing and AWS Marketplace is publishing your listing in AWS Marketplace.
- **Expired** – You started the request process, but did not complete within six months so the request expired.

Once all actions are completed for your listing, the request is moved to the **Request History** tab. Requests will have a status or **Published** or **Cancelled**. All published listings (as a limited listing or a published product) will appear under **Current Listings**. On the Self-Service Listings page, you can also view your current listings and download a pre-filled product load form for each listing.

If you have an entry with a status of **Submitted**, you can retract the submission. If you have an entry with a status of **In Draft**, you can delete the request. This will allow you to start over. When you delete an **In Draft** entry, the entry is moved to the **Request History** tab.

To list your product in the AWS GovCloud (U.S.) region, you need to have an active AWS GovCloud (U.S.) account and comply with the AWS GovCloud (U.S.) requirements, including export control requirements.

Submitting Products Using Self-Service Listings

You list most products using Self-Service Listings. To submit products using the SSL tool:

1. From the AMMP, choose the **Listings** tab.

2. In **Create a New Product**, use the pull-down menu to select a pricing model, and then choose **Create Product**. **Note**: monthly pricing is not supported in Self-Service Listings. For monthly pricing, use the Product Load Form.

3. Fill out the metadata fields in each of the tabs and submit the information to be reviewed by the AWS Marketplace Seller Operations team. Your product submission is reviewed for policy and security compliance, software vulnerabilities, and product usability prior to listing in AWS Marketplace. Once you have submitted your new product you can monitor the status of your submission through the SSL dashboard. When AWS Marketplace has approved your new listing's metadata submission, you will be provided with a link to review a limited version of your new product listing through the Self-Service Listings portal. After you review and approve your limited listing, your product listing will be published to the AWS Marketplace website and the limited listing removed.

Updating Products Using Self-Service Listings

The SSL tool is used to make one or more changes to the listings you created with the SSL tool. You can add a new version, remove existing versions, and update pricing, instance types, region availability, and metadata. To make an update, you prepare any updated product the same way you do new products. Once the product is prepared:

1. From the AWS Marketplace Management Portal, choose the **Listings** tab.

2. In **Current Listings**, locate the product you want to modify.

3. Under the **Actions** column (for the product you want to edit), use the **Select action** pull-down menu to choose the change you want to make.

4. Fill out the appropriate fields in each of the tabs and submit your change.

Your product submission is reviewed using a similar process to the one used when you create a new product. You can monitor the status of your submission using the SSL dashboard. After your product has been approved by the AWS Marketplace team your updates will be published live on the AWS Marketplace web site.

AWS CloudFormation-launched Product (free or paid) or Usage-based paid AMI product

Products that AWS Marketplace customer launch by using AWS CloudFormation templates must be submitted using the **Product Load Form** available through the AMMP.

Submitting Your Product

1. From the AMMP, download the Product Load Form for your product.

2. Add your product definition, which includes product information (title, description, highlights), technical information (AMI_ID, regions, instance types, OS), and pricing details (pricing model, Free Trial).

3. Submit your form following the instructions under the Instructions table of the spreadsheet.

AWS Marketplace reviews your product for policy and security compliance, software vulnerabilities, and product usability. If there are any questions or issues with a request, the AWS Marketplace team will contact you via email to discuss your request. Once approved, a mock-up of your listing page will be created. You review the listing and accept or reject the listing. Once approved, the listing will be added to the AWS Marketplace.

Updating Your Product

The Product Load Form is used to make one or more changes to the listings you created using the Product Load Form. You can make changes to the original product load form you completed, or, if not available you can start with a new load form. Just like using the SSL tool, you can add a new version, remove existing versions, and update pricing, instance types, region availability, and metadata. To make an update, you prepare any updated product the same way you do new products. Once the product is prepared:

1. Use your existing product load form, or, from the AWS Marketplace Management Portal, download the Product Load Form.

2. Update your product submission in the product load form.

3. From the AWS Marketplace Management Portal, Choose **File Upload**.

4. On the **File Uploads** page, upload your updated product load form and AWS CloudFormation templates. The file uploader provides a secure transfer mechanism and a history of submitted files. The uploader automatically notifies the AWS Marketplace team to begin processing your request. Include a description of the submission (adding new version, changing price, changing metadata, etc.).

Your product submission is reviewed for policy and security compliance, software vulnerabilities, and product usability. If there are any questions or issues with a request, the AWS Marketplace team will contact you via email. You do not review the updated listing prior to release to the AWS Marketplace. Updates to existing listings are processed and released directly to the AWS Marketplace.

Product Changes and Updates

Sellers can submit changes to their product at any time, and they will be processed as described above. However, some changes can only be made every 90 or 120 days, or when pending changes are in place. Examples include price changes, and region/instance type changes. Common changes include:

- **New Version -** New versions of the software, roll-outs of patches or updates. At your request, we can notify customers who have subscribed to Your Marketplace Content about the availability of new versions or send upgrade instructions on your behalf.
- **Metadata change** - Changes to product information (Description, URLs, and Usage Instructions).
- **Pricing Change** - A change to the pricing amount. A notification to current customers is sent once the request is complete.
- **Pricing Model Change** - A change to the pricing model (i.e. Hourly, Free, Hourly_Annual). Not all pricing model changes are supported and all requests to change models must be reviewed and approved by AWS Marketplace. **Note**: Any change from a free to a paid model presents significant impact to existing customers. An alternative is to propose a new listing with additional features and encourage current customers to migrate.
- **Region or Instance change** - Adding or removing instances types or regions.
- **Product takedown -** Remove a listing from AWS Marketplace to prevent new customers from subscribing. A notification to current customers is sent once the request is complete.

Timing and Expectations

While we strive to process requests as quickly as possible, requests can require multiple iterations and review by the seller and AWS Marketplace teams. Use the following as guidance for how long it will take to complete the process:

- Total request time normally takes **2-4 weeks of calendar time;** more complex requests or products can add additional time to allow for multiple iterations and adjustments to product metadata and software.
- Review and processing of requests typically requires **3 business days**. We will notify you if there are any issues that require additional action.
- We request a completed Product Form or Self-Service Listings request and AMI at least **45 days in advance** of any planned events or releases so we can prioritize the request accordingly.

If you have any questions about your request, contact AWS Marketplace Seller Operations at **aws-marketplace-seller-ops@amazon.com**.

Submitting AMIs to AWS Marketplace

ALL AMIs built and submitted to AWS Marketplace must adhere to all product policies. We suggest a few final checks of your AMI prior to submission:

- Remove all user credentials from the system; all default passwords, auth keys, key pairs, security keys or other credentials.
- Ensure that root login is disabled / locked; only sudo access accounts are allowed.
- If you are submitting an AMI to be deployed into the AWS GovCloud (US) region, you need to have an active AWS GovCloud account and agree to the AWS GovCloud Requirements, including applicable export control requirements.

AMI Self Service Scanning

Self-service AMI scanning is available within the AWS Marketplace Management Portal. With this feature, you can initiate scans of your AMIs and receive scanning results quickly – typically in less than an hour – with clear feedback in a single location.

To begin sharing and scanning your AMI with this new service:

1. Navigate to https://aws.amazon.com/marketplace/management/manage-products/

2. Select the AMI to share

3. View your scan results

Once your AMI has successfully been scanned, you can follow the current process to submit the AMI for processing by the AWS Marketplace Seller and Catalog Operations team by uploading your product load form or emailing **aws-marketplace-seller-ops@amazon.com**.

Please note that in order for your AMI to be included in the self-service AMI scanning list, it must be in the us-east-1 (N. Virginia) region and owned by your AWS Marketplace seller account. If you need additional accounts whitelisted for the AWS Marketplace Management Portal, please contact **aws-marketplace-seller-ops@amazon.com** with the AWS Account ID that owns the AMI to be scanned.

AMI Cloning and Product Code Assignment

Once your AMI is submitted, AWS Marketplace will create cloned AMIs for each region that you have indicated that software should be available. During this cloning and publishing process, AWS Marketplace will attach a product code to the cloned AMIs. The product code is used to both control access and to meter usage. All submissions must go through this AMI cloning process.

Final Checklist

Use this checklist prior to submitting your product listing to help avoid delays in publishing your listing.

Product usage

- Production-ready
- Does not restrict product usage by time or other restrictions
- Compatible with 1-click fulfillment experience
- Everything required to utilize the product is contained within the software including client applications
- Default user utilizes a randomized password and/or creation of initial user requires verification that the subscriber is authorized to use the instance using a value unique to the instance such as instance ID

For Free or Paid products:

- No additional license is required to use the product
- Subscriber does not have to provide personally identifiable information (e.g. email address) to use the product **AMI preparation**
- Utilizes hardware virtual machine (HVM) virtualization and 64-bit architecture
- Does not contain any known vulnerabilities, malware or viruses
- Subscribers have OS-level administration access to the AMI
- Run your AMI through AMI Self Service Scanning

For Windows AMIs:

- Utilizes the most recent version of Ec2ConfigService
- Ec2SetPassword, Ec2WindowsActiviate and Ec2HandleUserData are enabled
- No Guest Accounts or Remote Desktop Users are present

For Linux AMIs:

- Root login is locked/disabled
- No authorized keys, default passwords or other credentials are included **Load form or Self-service listings preparation**
- All required fields are completed
- All values are within specified character limits
- All URLs load without error
- Product image is at least 110px wide and between a 1:1 and 2:1 ratio
- Pricing is specified for all enabled instance types (for hourly, hourly_monthly and hourly_annual pricing models)
- Monthly pricing is specified (for hourly_monthly and monthly pricing models)

If you have any questions or comments about automated AMI building, please contact **aws-marketplace-seller-ops@amazon.com**

AWS Marketplace Seller Reports

AWS Marketplace provides you the ability to retrieve reports for your listings. The information available includes data on your listings, customers, financials, usage, and any U.S. Sales and Use Tax collected for use of your software. Different reports provide data covering daily and monthly time periods. All reports are generated as .csv files so you can open with a variety of tools, or import into other systems. You can download and view sample reports here.

AWS Marketplace strives to deliver as much data as possible to allow your listings and business to be successful on AWS Marketplace, we also adhere to strict Amazon standards and tenets around protecting customer data and not sharing personally identifiable information. We will sometimes obfuscate or genericize customer data or specific details.

Accessing Your Reports

AWS Marketplace provides you two ways to obtain your reports:

1. Use the AWS Marketplace Commerce Analytics Service to request reports via API and retrieve them from an S3 bucket.

2. Access and download reports on the AWS Marketplace Management Portal under the Reports tab.

To protect customer privacy and trust, we do not share individually-identifying customer information such as email addresses. However, for sales compensation purposes we share certain entity-level information about your customers through the AWS Marketplace Enhanced Data Sharing Program. If you have enabled AWS Marketplace Product Support Connection for your products, customers who purchase your products can elect to share contact information with you that can be used for support purposes.

Reports via CAS

AWS Marketplace Commerce Analytics Service (CAS) allows you to programmatically access your AWS Marketplace data via an API interface. The interface provides you a way to automate the download and data ingestion of your information. We highly recommend this method for accessing your AWS Marketplace data.

Reports via Portal

All AWS Marketplace reports are available for download in the AWS Marketplace Management Portal, including reports for prior reporting periods. Report notifications will be sent to the email address associated with the AWS account you registered with to sell on AWS Marketplace.

Report Types

There are several reports available to track daily and monthly data. Included in the reports is information about usage that has been billed to AWS customers, information about payment received from customers, and money being disbursed to you. Disbursement does not occur until payment is received from the AWS customer. Description of common terms:

Billed – AWS customers are billed at the beginning of every month for the metered usage incurred in the previous month. Customers are also billed immediately when they purchase annual AMI subscriptions or SaaS contracts.

Payment – Payment is due immediately for AWS customers who pay with a credit card. Some customers have other payment arrangements with AWS billing that can change when their payment is due. For instance, those that are invoiced.

Disbursement – Payments from AWS customers are disbursed to you every month of a regular cycle, and the reporting for disbursements is available to you a few days later.

The table below provides an overview of the types of reports and their purpose. We recommend you download and view the sample reports.

Report Name	Description
Daily Customer Subscriber Report	This report tells you the AWS account ID of every customer subscribed to your products, including the number of current and new annual subscriptions for each day.
Daily Business Report	This report provide information on daily usage by AWS customers, and projects the estimated revenue expected from customer usage.
Monthly Billed Revenue Report	This is a monthly report which gives you the revenue that has been billed to customers for usage of your software product as a result of hourly usage, or annual and monthly fees incurred.
Monthly Disbursement Report	This report breaks down money collected and disbursed to you for usage of your software product since your previous disbursement.
U.S. Sales and Use Tax Report	This is part of the AWS Marketplace Tax Calculation Service and reports on U.S. sales and use taxes calculated for your products.
Daily Ref Tag (dashboard)	This report references the same information from your Marketing Dashboard, providing insight into clicks and conversions for your ref tag links.
Weekly Ref Tag (dashboard)	This is a weekly summary of your product's ref tag data, and the clicks and conversions associated with them.

Daily Customer Subscription Report

This report is available daily and tells you every AWS account ID which is subscribed to your products, including the number of current and new annual subscriptions for each day. Note that this report does not specify current or past usage, only that a customer is subscribed to your listing.

Daily Business Report

This report helps AWS Marketplace sellers understand how their products are being used by AWS customers on a daily basis, and projects the estimated revenue expected from that usage. The data in this report includes a unique identifier per customer (not the AWS Account Number) that can be used to identify an AWS customer across report types and across days. Sellers can track customer usage patterns and estimated customer spend with this ID, as well as gain insights into free trial and annual data.

Monthly Billed Revenue

This is a report on a monthly cadence which gives you the revenue that has been billed to the customers for usage of your software product as a result of hourly usage, or annual and monthly fees incurred. Please note that the amounts in this report reflect revenue billed to customers, not amounts actually collected from customers.

Disbursement Report

This monthly report breaks down money received from customers and disbursed to you.

Uncollected Funds FAQ

Q: What does "Uncollected mean in my Disbursement Report?

A: The amount not paid yet by customers (during the specified timeframe).

Q: Why are there uncollected amounts listed in my report and when will they be disbursed?

A: We can only disburse money that was successfully collected from subscribers. Once funds are collected, they will be disbursed at the next settlement date. Please also note that some customers are on different payment terms.

Q: Why are there discrepancies between the Monthly Billing (Revenue Report) and Disbursement?

A: The Monthly Billing Report shows you how subscribers are changing within a given week (new, current, and cancelled). It's really a snapshot of activity. The disbursement report gives you details on fees that we successfully collected and disbursed to you in a given reporting period. The following things can affect Billing vs. Disbursement:

- Some of our larger customers are on net terms, meaning that while they consume services in one month, the actual fees will only be collected in the following month(s).
- Payments for customers on credit cards can fall through if a customer fails to update credit card details in our systems or credit cards becoming invalid. Those fees will show up as uncollected.

Q: What steps does AWS take to address the issue of non-paying users?

A: AWS takes several steps to follow-up with customers on their payment, and will take action on accounts that are determined to be delinquent.

Q: How does a customer end up on different net terms?

A: AWS customers must go through a thorough approval process which includes a review of how much they're spending, payment history, and credit checks.

U.S. Sales and Use Tax Report

This monthly report provides sellers with information about U.S. sales and use taxes calculated by Amazon from transactions in AWS Marketplace. You will only receive this report if you enroll in the AWS Marketplace Tax Calculation Service. The report includes calculated U.S. sales and use tax for products that have a Product Tax Code applied. Any products without a Product Tax Code will appear in this report with a tax value of $0.00.

To identify whether tax funds were collected, you should refer to your monthly Disbursement Report. Transactions can be mapped between the Disbursement Report and U.S. Sales and Use Tax Report by using the shared Transaction Reference ID.

Daily Ref Tag

This report presents the information from your Marketing Dashboard and provides insight into clicks and conversions for ref tag links that customers use to get to your AWS Marketplace listing.

- The report covers the previous 24 hour calendar period, and is can be downloaded from the Marketing Dashboard of your AWS Marketplace Management Portal.
- This report is not emailed.

- Video for Getting Started with AWS Marketplace Marketing Analytics.
- Additional help on setting up ref tags.
- You cannot make calls to the Commerce Analytics Service (CAS) for this report.
- The filename is formatted as reftag_daily_breakdown_report_YYYY-MM-DD.csv where the date is the date the report was generated.

The report contains 1 section relating to customer billing activity:

1. Clicks and Conversions - A breakdown of every ref tag used with your products and the amount of clicks, conversions, estimated usage, and estimated revenue associated with them.

Weekly Ref Tag

This report presents the information from your Marketing Dashboard, summarized by week, and provides insight into clicks and conversions for ref tag links that customers use to get to your AWS Marketplace listing. The query used to generate your reftag reports looks for distinct customer sessions (grouped by day, reftag, and page ASIN) and reports them as clicks. The report does not measure conversion to paid.

- The report covers the previous 7 Day calendar period, and is normally generated and available weekly, usually by 5:00pm PST (Midnight UTC). The specific period covered is included in the report.
- Video for Getting Started with AWS Marketplace Marketing Analytics.
- Additional help on setting up ref tags.
- You cannot make calls to the Commerce Analytics Service (CAS) for this report.
- Please note only ref tags that contain '_ptnr_' are included in this report plus any SEM/Online ad ref tags that start with 'ads_'.
- The filename is formatted as weekly_reftag_report_YYYY-MM-DD.csv where the date is the date the report was generated.

The report contains 1 section relating to customer billing activity:

1. Clicks and Conversions - A breakdown of every ref tag used with your products and the amount of clicks and conversions associated with them.

Reporting Frequently Asked Questions (FAQ)

General

Q: How can others from my team access reports in the AWS Marketplace Management Portal?

A: You can control access to the AWS Marketplace Management Portal using IAM users.

Q: Can we unsubscribe from new report email notifications?

A: Yes you can. Send your request for cancel your subscription to **aws-marketplace-seller-ops@amazon.com**.

Q: Why didn't I receive a Daily Customer Subscriber or Daily Business Report today?

A: Reports are only generated when there is relevant data available that our system can enter in to them. For example, if you have no subscribers on any of your products, then the Daily Customer Subscriber report won't be generated. If you still believe this is an error, contact **aws-marketplace-seller-ops@amazon.com** and the team will investigate.

Q: Can you share more information about customers?

A: No. Refer to the AWS Marketplace Enhanced Data Sharing Program documentation for more information.

Q: Can I run my own custom reports?

A: No, this is not a currently supported feature. However, you can use the AWS Marketplace Commerce Analytics Service API to download report data in a machine-readable format.

Q: What is Refund in the Disbursement Report?

A: Refund represents money returned from the seller to the customer. It's represented as a negative amount since the money is deducted from the total disbursement amount.

Q: How can I tell which entries are for private offers?

A: Offer ID and **Offer Visibility** columns have been added to reports to help distinguish private offer entries.

**Q. How is the US sales tax handled? **

A. For more information about AWS Marketplace's Tax Calculation Service, please visit the AWS Marketplace Management Portal's Settings page.

Q: Can a customer split a bill across several credit cards or do a direct invoicing?

A: For pro-rated Monthly fees, customers can do both split payments and direct invoicing. However, for Annual subscriptions, customers can only do direct invoicing.

Q: Can I download past reports?

A: You have access to past reports on management portal. If you don't see the report there, contact **aws-marketplace-seller-ops@amazon.com** and we will look into it.

Q: Do reports include BYOL products?

A: Information about your BYOL products are included in your Daily Business Report.

Q: Reftag Report - How are clicks measured from your system?

A: When you provide us with a reftag on the AWS Marketplace website, the reftag data is measured and recorded into logs. These logs are then loaded into a table which is then queried on a daily basis.

Q: Reftag Report - If I spin up an instance remotely from my product's GUI or using an API, does your reporting account for that instance (AMI) and can I attribute that by the campaign? Or is the AMI instance only recorded when executed from the AWS console?

A: We only track clicks and conversions made by the customer from the AWS Marketplace website.

Commerce Analytics Service (CAS)

Q: What are the benefits of the AWS Marketplace Commerce Analytics Service?

A: This new service allows you to programmatically access your AWS Marketplace data, removing the need for the inconvenient and potentially error-prone process of manually downloading and processing reports from the AWS Marketplace Management Portal website. Now, you can retrieve your products' usage, subscribers, disbursement, and payment information using a modern API interface that allows you to automate the download and data ingestion of your information.

Q: What is the difference between the Commerce Analytics Service and a traditional API?

A: The Commerce Analytics Service programmatically returns data asynchronously to a file in S3 rather than directly like a traditional API. This is because of the nature of the data being potentially large and unbounded. When the data has been delivered to your S3 bucket, we'll send you a notification using Amazon Simple Notification Service (SNS).

Q: What will happen to the existing reports on the AWS Marketplace Management Portal website?

A: The current reports will remain accessible from the AWS Marketplace Management Portal website. There are currently no plans to remove these reports. In the future, as sellers fully integrate with the new service, we may consider retiring the existing reports.

Q: What are the requirements to start utilizing the service?

A: You must be an active seller in the AWS Marketplace and you must enroll in the program through the AWS Marketplace Management Portal. From the Management Portal, navigate to the Reports tab and follow the on-screen instructions.

Q: What work will be required of my company to take advantage of the data provided in the AWS Marketplace Commerce Analytics Service?

A: In order to automate your access to AWS Marketplace data, one of your technical resources needs to use the AWS Software Development Kit (SDK) to communicate with the AWS Marketplace Commerce Analytics Service. The SDK supports multiple programming platforms such as .NET, Java, Ruby, Command Line Interface, and many more.

Q: What can I do with the data provided in the AWS Marketplace Commerce Analytics Service?

A: Data published by the Commerce Analytics Service is in a machine-readable format, making it easy for you to import it into your existing systems, databases, or business intelligence and data analysis software. You can also directly manipulate the data from the service, allowing you to aggregate and augment the data with your own internal data.

Enhanced Data Sharing

If you wish to receive de-obfuscated customer information for the purpose of compensating your sales team for sales of products via AWS Marketplace, AWS Marketplace offers an additional Sales Compensation report. Sales Compensation reports contain additional information such as customer email domain, customer AWS Account ID, and location in order to help you compensate your field, and use of such information is strictly limited to field sales team compensation.

For more information about program requirements and how to sign up to receive this data, please review the AWS Marketplace Enhanced Data Sharing Program Guide.

Daily Business Report

This document is designed to help AWS Marketplace sellers understand the reports they receive on a daily and monthly cadence. The document examines each report, and defines its purpose and the data elements in the report.

This report helps sellers understand how their products are being used by AWS customers on a daily basis and projects the estimated revenue expected from that usage. The data in this report includes a unique identifier per customer that can be used to identify an AWS customer across report types and across days. Sellers can track customer usage patterns and estimated customer spend with this ID, as well as gain insights into free trial and annual data. This report has six sections and we will look at the data elements in each section below.

Publication Schedule

Daily, by 5:00 PM Pacific Time.

Section 1: Usage by Instance Type

Data Coverage Period

Includes data from the 24-hour period of the previous day.

Column Name	Available for all sellers	Available for sellers enrolled in the Enhanced Data Sharing program	Description
Customer Reference ID			A unique ID (not AWS Account Number) associated with the AWS account subscribed to the product to help track usage, revenue and subscriptions by customers
User's State			The billing address state associated with the AWS account subscribed to the product
User's Country			The billing address country associated with the AWS account subscribed to the product
Product Title			The title of the product
Product Code			A unique identifier representing the individual software product
Instance Type			The instance type associated with usage (e.g. t2.micro)

Column Name	Available for all sellers	Available for sellers enrolled in the Enhanced Data Sharing program	Description
Usage Units			The number of units of usage associated with the product
Usage Unit Type			The usage units associated with the usage unit count (e.g. hours)
Offering Description			The description of how the product is being offered (e.g. hourly, free trial, annual)
Estimated Revenue			The estimated revenue resulting from associated usage. This is 'estimated' as the billing is finalized at the end of the month
Currency			The currency (e.g. USD) associated with the estimated revenue
Offer ID			The identifier for the offer the subscriber signed
Offer Visibility			Indicates the offer to be a public, private, or enterprise contract offer
Customer AWS Account Number			The AWS account number-- associated with the AWS account to which software charges are billed
Customer Country			The billin-g address country associated with the AWS account to which software charges are billed
Customer State			The billing address state associated with the AWS account to which software charges are billed
Customer City			The billing address city associated with the AWS account to which software charges are billed

Column Name	Available for all sellers	Available for sellers enrolled in the Enhanced Data Sharing program	Description
Customer Zip Code			The billing address zip code associated with the AWS account to which software charges are billed
Customer Email Domain			The email domain associated with the AWS account to which software charges are billed, e.g. "amazon.com"
Solution Title			The name of the solution
Solution ID			The unique identifier for the solution

Section 2: Fees

This section includes fee-based transactions, including Annual, Monthly, and SaaS Contracts products.

Data Coverage Period

Includes data from the 24-hour period occurring 72-hours before the report was published.

Column Name	Available for all sellers	Available for sellers enrolled in the Enhanced Data Sharing program	Description
Customer Reference ID			A unique ID (not AWS Account Number) associated with the AWS account subscribed to the product to help track usage, revenue and subscriptions by customers
User's State			The billing address state associated with the AWS account subscribed to the product
User's Country			The billing address country associated with the AWS account subscribed to the product
Product Title			The title of the product

Column Name	Available for all sellers	Available for sellers enrolled in the Enhanced Data Sharing program	Description
Product Code			A unique identifier representing the individual software product
Amount			The software usage fee. If there is a refund, this value will be negative. If this entry is for an AWS Marketplace SaaS contract, the amount represents the software fee for the dimension, not the entire contract.
Currency			The currency (e.g. USD) associated with the estimated revenue
Fee Description			The reason for the fee (e.g. monthly fee, annual fee, SaaS Contracts fee, refund, etc.)
Customer AWS Account Number			The AWS account number-- associated with the AWS account to which software charges are billed
Customer Country			The billin-g address country associated with the AWS account to which software charges are billed
Customer State			The billing address state associated with the AWS account to which software charges are billed
Customer City			The billing address city associated with the AWS account to which software charges are billed
Customer Zip Code			The billing address zip code associated with the AWS account to which software charges are billed
Customer Email Domain			The email domain associated with the AWS account to which software charges are billed, e.g. "amazon.com"

Column Name	Available for all sellers	Available for sellers enrolled in the Enhanced Data Sharing program	Description
Start Date			The start date for an AWS Marketplace SaaS contract
End Date			The end date for an AWS Marketplace SaaS contract
Quantity			The number of units for a dimension specified in the contract
Dimension			The dimension specified in the contract
Solution Title			The name of the solution
Solution ID			The unique identifier for the solution

Section 3: Free Trial Conversions

Data Coverage Period

Includes data from the 24-hour period of the previous day.

Column Name	Available for all sellers	Available for sellers enrolled in the Enhanced Data Sharing program	Description
Product Title			The title of the product
Product Code			A unique identifier representing the individual software product
New Free Trials			The count of the new free trials initiated that day
Total Current Free Trials			The total count of all active free trial subscriptions
Converted Free Trials			The total count of subscriptions that moved from free trial to paid usage that day
Non-Converted Free Trials			The total count of the total subscriptions that ended the free trial and did not convert to paid usage
Solution Title			The name of the solution

Column Name	Available for all sellers	Available for sellers enrolled in the Enhanced Data Sharing program	Description
Solution ID			The unique identifier for the solution

Section 4: New Instances

Data Coverage Period

Includes data from the 24-hour period of the previous day.

Column Name	Available for all sellers	Available for sellers enrolled in the Enhanced Data Sharing program	Description
Customer Reference ID			A unique ID (not AWS Account Number) associated with the AWS account subscribed to the product to help track usage, revenue and subscriptions by customers
User's State			The billing address state associated with the AWS account subscribed to the product
User's Country			The billing address country associated with the AWS account subscribed to the product
Product Title			The title of the product
Product Code			A unique identifier representing the individual software product
Type			The AWS EC2 instance type
Count			The count of AWS EC2 instances
Customer AWS Account Number			The AWS account number-- associated with the AWS account to which software charges are billed

Column Name	Available for all sellers	Available for sellers enrolled in the Enhanced Data Sharing program	Description
Customer Country			The billin-g address country associated with the AWS account to which software charges are billed
Customer State			The billing address state associated with the AWS account to which software charges are billed
Customer City			The billing address city associated with the AWS account to which software charges are billed
Customer Zip Code			The billing address zip code associated with the AWS account to which software charges are billed
Customer Email Domain			The email domain associated with the AWS account to which software charges are billed, e.g. "amazon.com"
Solution Title			The name of the solution
Solution ID			The unique identifier for the solution

Section 5: New Product Subscribers

Data Coverage Period

Includes data from the 24-hour period of the previous day.

Column Name	Available for all sellers	Available for sellers enrolled in the Enhanced Data Sharing program	Description
Customer Reference ID			A unique ID (not AWS Account Number) associated with the AWS account subscribed to the product to help track usage, revenue and subscriptions by customers

Column Name	Available for all sellers	Available for sellers enrolled in the Enhanced Data Sharing program	Description
User's State			The billing address state associated with the AWS account subscribed to the product
User's Country			The billing address country associated with the AWS account subscribed to the product
Product Title			The title of the product
Product Code			A unique identifier representing the individual software product
Offer ID			The identifier for the offer the subscriber signed
Offer Visibility			Indicates the offer to be a public, private, or enterprise contract offer
Customer Country			The billing address country associated with the AWS account to which software charges are billed
Customer State			The billing address state associated with the AWS account to which software charges are billed
Customer City			The billing address city associated with the AWS account to which software charges are billed
Customer Zip Code			The billing address zip code associated with the AWS account to which software charges are billed
Customer Email Domain			The email domain associated with the AWS account to which software charges are billed, e.g. "amazon.com"
Solution Title			The name of the solution

Column Name	Available for all sellers	Available for sellers enrolled in the Enhanced Data Sharing program	Description
Solution ID			The unique identifier for the solution

Section 6: Canceled Product Subscribers

Data Coverage Period

Includes data from the 24-hour period of the previous day.

Column Name	Available for all sellers	Available for sellers enrolled in the Enhanced Data Sharing program	Description
Customer Reference ID			A unique ID (not AWS Account Number) associated with the AWS account subscribed to the product to help track usage, revenue and subscriptions by customers
User's State			The billing address state associated with the AWS account subscribed to the product
User's Country			The billing address country associated with the AWS account subscribed to the product
Product Title			The title of the product
Product Code			A unique identifier representing the individual software product
Subscribed Date			The date when the subscription started
Offer ID			The identifier for the offer the subscriber signed
Offer Visibility			Indicates the offer to be a public, private, or enterprise contract offer

Column Name	Available for all sellers	Available for sellers enrolled in the Enhanced Data Sharing program	Description
Customer AWS Account Number			The AWS account number-- associated with the AWS account to which software charges are billed
Customer Country			The billin-g address country associated with the AWS account to which software charges are billed
Customer State			The billing address state associated with the AWS account to which software charges are billed
Customer City			The billing address city associated with the AWS account to which software charges are billed
Customer Zip Code			The billing address zip code associated with the AWS account to which software charges are billed
Customer Email Domain			The email domain associated with the AWS account to which software charges are billed, e.g. "amazon.com"
Solution Title			The name of the solution
Solution ID			The unique identifier for the solution

Daily Customer Subscriber Report

This report gives sellers a list of AWS Account IDs for all customers currently subscribed to their products.

Publication Schedule

Daily, by 5:00 PM Pacific Time.

Section 1: Hourly/Monthly subscriptions

Data Coverage Period

Includes all usage-based subscriptions as of the previous day at 23:59:59 UTC.

Column Name	Description
Customer AWS Account Number	The AWS account number-- associated with the AWS account which is subscribed to the to the listing. This is a 12-digit number, represented by 3 sets of 4 numbers, separated by hyphens, e.g. 1234-5678-9012
Product Title	The title of the product
Product Id	A unique identifier representing the individual software product
Product Code	A unique identifier representing the individual software product, which is also available in EC2 Instance Metadata
Subscription Start Date	The date when the customer subscribed to the listing, formatted as YYYY-MM-DD
Offer ID	The identifier for the offer the subscriber signed
Offer Visibility	Indicates the offer to be a public, private, or enterprise contract offer
Solution Title	The name of the solution
Solution ID	The unique identifier for the solution

Section 2: Annual subscriptions

Data Coverage Period

Includes all fee-based subscriptions as of the previous day at 23:59:59 UTC.

Column Name	Description
Customer AWS Account Number	The AWS account number-- associated with the AWS account which is subscribed to the to the listing. This is a 12-digit number, represented by 3 sets of 4 numbers, separated by hyphens, e.g. 1234-5678-9012
Product Title	The title of the product
Product Id	A unique identifier representing the individual software product

Column Name	Description
Product Code	A unique identifier representing the individual software product, which is also available in EC2 Instance Metadata
Annual Subscription Id	The ID of the annual subscription
Annual Subscription Quantity	The total number of licenses the customer specified as part of the annual purchase
Annual Subscription Type	The type of annual subscription
Subscription Start Date	The date when the customer subscribed to the listing, formatted as YYYY-MM-DD
Offer ID	The identifier for the offer the subscriber signed
Offer Visibility	Indicates the offer to be a public, private, or enterprise contract offer
Solution Title	The name of the solution
Solution ID	The unique identifier for the solution

Monthly Billed Revenue Report

This report is designed to provide sellers with authoritative information about billed revenue every month for accounting and other financial reporting purposes. This report shows the total amounts billed to customers by AWS for hourly, annual, or monthly usage of your software. **The amounts in this report only reflect revenue billed to customers, and not amounts actually collected.**

There are two sections in this report. Section 1 shows the billed amount for hourly usage and monthly fees, and section 2 shows the annual subscriptions and billed amount for those subscriptions. Sellers can use the annual information to amortize as per their standards when reporting revenue.

Publication Schedule

Monthly, on the 15th of the month, by 5:00 PM Pacific Time.

Section 1: Billing and Revenue Data

Data Coverage Period

Includes usage-based software charges from the previous calendar month.

Column Name	Available for all sellers	Available for sellers enrolled in the Enhanced Data Sharing program	Description
Customer Reference ID			A unique ID (not AWS Account Number) associated with the AWS account to which fees are billed, to help track usage, revenue, and subscriptions by customers
Country			The billin-g address country associated with the AWS account to which software charges are billed
State			The billing address state associated with the AWS account to which software charges are billed
City			The billing address city associated with the AWS account to which software charges are billed

Column Name	Available for all sellers	Available for sellers enrolled in the Enhanced Data Sharing program	Description
Zip Code			The billing address zip code associated with the AWS account to which software charges are billed
Product Title			The title of the product
Product Code			A unique identifier representing the individual software product
Customer Billed Amount			The amount billed for the usage or monthly fees
AWS Fee			The AWS listing fee amount that will be deducted from the billed amount
Refunds Amount			The total amount refunded (if applicable)
AWS Fee Refund			The portion of the AWS Marketplace listing fee refunded (if applicable)
Partner Revenue Amount			The total amount billed for the transaction, net of AWS Marketplace listing fees, refunds, and U.S. sales and use tax.
Currency			The currency (e.g. USD)
Transaction Reference ID			A unique identifier representing the transaction which can be used to correlate transactions across AWS Marketplace reports
U.S. Sales Tax Customer Billed Amount			The total amount of U.S. sales and use tax billed for this transaction
U.S. Sales Tax Refunds Amount			The total amount of U.S. sales and use tax refunded for this transaction (if applicable)
Offer ID			The identifier for the offer the subscriber signed

Column Name	Available for all sellers	Available for sellers enrolled in the Enhanced Data Sharing program	Description
Offer Visibility			Indicates the offer to be a public, private, or enterprise contract offer
Customer AWS Account Number			The AWS account number-- associated with the AWS account to which software charges are billed
Customer Email Domain			The email domain associated with the AWS account to which software charges are billed, e.g. "amazon.com"
Opportunity Name			The unique identifier for a registered opportunity.
Opportunity Description			Metadata for the registered opportunity.
Solution Title			The name of the solution
Solution ID			The unique identifier for the solution

Section 2: Annual Subscriptions

Data Coverage Period

Includes fee-based software charges from the previous calendar month.

Column Name	Available for all sellers	Available for sellers enrolled in the Enhanced Data Sharing program	Description
Customer Reference ID			A unique ID (not AWS Account Number) associated with the AWS account to which fees are billed, to help track usage, revenue, and subscriptions by customers
Country			The billin-g address country associated with the AWS account to which software charges are billed

Column Name	Available for all sellers	Available for sellers enrolled in the Enhanced Data Sharing program	Description
State			The billing address state associated with the AWS account to which software charges are billed
City			The billing address city associated with the AWS account to which software charges are billed
Zip Code			The billing address zip code associated with the AWS account to which software charges are billed
Product Title			The title of the product
Product Code			A unique identifier representing the individual software product
Annual Subscription Quantity			The count of total licenses specified as part of the annual purchase
Annual Subscription Start Date			The start date of the annual purchase
Annual Subscription End Date			The end date of the annual purchase
Annual Subscription Instance Type			The instance type associated with the annual purchase
Customer Billed Amount			The amount billed for the usage or monthly fees
AWS Fee			The AWS Marketplace listing fee amount that will be deducted from the billed amount
Refunds Amount			The total amount refunded (if applicable)
AWS Fee Refund			The portion of the AWS Marketplace listing fee refunded (if applicable)
Partner Revenue Amount			The total amount billed for this transaction, net of AWS Marketplace listing fees, refunds, and U.S. sales and use tax.

Column Name	Available for all sellers	Available for sellers enrolled in the Enhanced Data Sharing program	Description
Currency			The currency (e.g. USD)
Transaction Reference ID			A unique identifier representing the transaction which can be used to correlate transactions across AWS Marketplace reports
U.S. Sales Tax Customer Billed Amount			The total amount of U.S. sales and use tax billed for this transaction
U.S. Sales Tax Refunds Amount			The total amount of U.S. sales and use tax refunded for this transaction (if applicable)
Customer AWS Account Number			The AWS account number-- associated with the AWS account to which software charges are billed
Customer Email Domain			The email domain associated with the AWS account to which software charges are billed, e.g. "amazon.com"
Offer ID			The identifier for the offer the subscriber signed
Offer Visibility			Indicates the offer to be a public, private, or enterprise contract offer
Contract Start Date			The start date for an AWS Marketplace SaaS contract
Contract End Date			The end date for an AWS Marketplace SaaS contract
Opportunity Name			The unique identifier for a registered opportunity.
Opportunity Description			Metadata for the registered opportunity.
Solution Title			The name of the solution
Solution ID			The unique identifier for the solution

Section 3: AWS Field Demonstration Usage

Data Coverage Period

Includes field demonstration usage from the previous calendar month.

Column Name	Available for all sellers	Available for sellers enrolled in the Enhanced Data Sharing program	Description
Product Title			The name of the product
Product Code			A unique identifier representing the individual software product
Instance Type			The instance type associated with the field demonstration
Usage Units			The number of units of usage associated with the product
Usage Unit Types			The usage units associated with the usage unit count (e.g. hours)

Monthly Disbursement Report

The Monthly Disbursement Report provides information about funds that have been collected and disbursed to sellers' bank accounts since the previous disbursement.

Publication Schedule

Monthly, 3 days after a successful disbursement by 5:00 PM Pacific Time.

Note: Disbursements to your bank account typically occur between the 7th and 10th of each month, so the Monthly Disbursement Report is typically published between the 10th and 13th of each month.

Section 1: Disbursed Amount by Product

Data Coverage Period

Includes funds which were collected since the previous monthly disbursement.

Column Name	Available for all sellers	Available for sellers enrolled in the Enhanced Data Sharing program	Description
Product			The title of the product
Product Code			A unique identifier representing the individual software product
SellerRev			The total software charge billed to the customer
AWSRefFee			The AWS Marketplace listing fee
SellerRevRefund			The total software charge refunded (if applicable)
AWSRefFeeRefund			The total AWS Marketplace listing fee refunded (if applicable)
SellerRevCredit			AWS credits placed onto the customer account by AWS Marketplace (if applicable)
AWSRefFeeCredit			AWS credits placed onto the seller account by AWS Marketplace (if applicable)
Net Amount			The total funds disbursed to the seller, less AWS Marketplace listing fees, refunds, and U.S. sales and use tax

Column Name	Available for all sellers	Available for sellers enrolled in the Enhanced Data Sharing program	Description
Transaction Reference ID			A unique identifier representing the transaction which can be used to correlate transactions across AWS Marketplace reports
SellerUSSalesTax			The total amount of U.S. sales and use tax disbursed to the seller for the transaction
SellerUSSalesTaxRe-fund			The total amount of U.S. sales and use tax refunded to the customer for the transaction (if applicable).
Customer AWS Account Number			The AWS account number-- associated with the AWS account to which software charges are billed
Customer Country			The billin-g address country associated with the AWS account to which software charges are billed
Customer State			The billing address state associated with the AWS account to which software charges are billed
Customer City			The billing address city associated with the AWS account to which software charges are billed
Customer Zip Code			The billing address zip code associated with the AWS account to which software charges are billed
Customer Email Domain			The email domain associated with the AWS account to which software charges are billed, e.g. "amazon.com"
Solution Title			The name of the solution
Solution ID			The unique identifier for the solution

Section 2: Disbursed Amount by Customer Geography

Data Coverage Period

Includes funds which were collected since the previous monthly disbursement.

Column Name	Available for all sellers	Available for sellers enrolled in the Enhanced Data Sharing program	Description
Settlement ID			The unique identifier of the disbursement
Settlement Period Start Date			The start date/time of the disbursement period
Settlement Period End Date			The end date/time of the disbursement period
Deposit Date			The date/time when the disbursement occurred
Disbursed Amount			The total amount of the disbursement
Country Code			The billin-g address country associated with the AWS account to which software charges are billed
State or Region			The billing address state associated with the AWS account to which software charges are billed
City			The billing address city associated with the AWS account to which software charges are billed
Postal Code			The billing address zip code associated with the AWS account to which software charges are billed
Net Amount by Tax Location			The total funds disbursed to the seller, less AWS Marketplace listing fees, refunds, and U.S. sales and use tax, grouped by location

Column Name	Available for all sellers	Available for sellers enrolled in the Enhanced Data Sharing program	Description
Gross Amount by Tax Location			The total funds disbursed to the seller, less AWS Marketplace listing fees, refunds, and U.S. sales and use tax, grouped by location
Seller U.S. Sales Tax			The total amount of U.S. sales and use tax disbursed to the seller for the transaction, grouped by location
Seller U.S. Sales Tax Refund			The total amount of U.S. sales and use tax refunded to the customer for the transaction (if applicable), grouped by location

Section 3: Disbursed Amount by Instance Hours

Data Coverage Period

Includes funds which were collected since the previous monthly disbursement.

Column Name	Available for all sellers	Available for sellers enrolled in the Enhanced Data Sharing program	Description
Product			The title of the product
Product Code			A unique identifier representing the individual software product
Usage Type Description			The description of the usage, including offer type, region, and instance type
Rate			The software rate per hour for this offer type, region, and instance type
User Count			The number of unique customers using this offer type, region, and instance type

Column Name	Available for all sellers	Available for sellers enrolled in the Enhanced Data Sharing program	Description
Instance Hours			The number of hours consumed for this offer type, region, and instance type
Solution Title			The name of the solution
Solution ID			The unique identifier for the solution

Section 4: Age of Uncollected Funds

Data Coverage Period

Includes funds which were collected since the previous monthly disbursement.

Column Name	Available for all sellers	Available for sellers enrolled in the Enhanced Data Sharing program	Description
Uncollected (< 31 days pending)			The total of uncollected funds less than 31 days pending. Note: "Uncollected" funds may include amounts that are not yet due.
Uncollected (31-60 days pending)			The total of uncollected funds between 31-60 days pending. Note: "Uncollected" funds may include amounts that are not yet due.
Uncollected (61-90 days pending)			The total of uncollected funds between 61-90 days pending. Note: "Uncollected" funds may include amounts that are not yet due.
Uncollected (91-120 days pending)			The total of uncollected funds between 91-120 days pending. Note: "Uncollected" funds may include amounts that are not yet due.

95

Column Name	Available for all sellers	Available for sellers enrolled in the Enhanced Data Sharing program	Description
Uncollected (> 120 days pending)			The total of uncollected funds greater than 120 days pending. Note: "Uncollected" funds may include amounts that are not yet due.
Uncollected (overall)			The total of all uncollected funds. "Uncollected" funds may include amounts that are not yet due.

Section 5: Age of Disbursed Funds

Data Coverage Period

Includes funds which were collected since the previous monthly disbursement.

Column Name	Available for all sellers	Available for sellers enrolled in the Enhanced Data Sharing program	Description
Collected (< 31 days pending)			The total of collected funds less than 31 days pending.
Collected (31-60 days pending)			The total of collected funds between 31-60 days pending.
Collected (61-90 days pending)			The total of collected funds between 61-90 days pending.
Collected (91-120 days pending)			The total of collected funds between 91-120 days pending.
Collected (> 120 days pending)			The total of collected funds greater than 120 days pending.
Collected (overall)			The total of all collected funds.

Sales Compensation Report

The Sales Compensation Report, which is available to sellers who participate in the Enhanced Data Sharing program, provides monthly billed revenue with additional customer information not found in the standard Monthly Billed Revenue report. This report shows the total amounts billed to customers by AWS for hourly, annual, or monthly usage of your software. **The amounts in this report only reflect revenue billed to customers, and not amounts actually collected.**

The Sales Compensation report, and the information being shared with you as part of this program, constitute Amazon's Confidential Information under our nondisclosure agreement with you or, if no such agreement exists, the Terms and Conditions for AWS Marketplace Sellers. It is to be used solely for the purpose of compensating your sales reps by mapping AWS Marketplace revenue to your sales reps by company name, geo and AWS Account ID. You may use such information for the foregoing purpose, including by sharing such information with employees who have a need to know such information to understand the source of commissions payable to them, provided that your use and sharing of such information complies with the obligations in the agreements specified above, including, without limitation, Section 3.8 of the Terms and Conditions for AWS Marketplace Sellers.

Publication Schedule

Monthly, on the 15th of the month, by 5:00 PM Pacific Time.

Section 1: Billed Revenue

Data Coverage Period

Includes usage and fee-based software charges from the previous calendar month.

Column Name	Description
Customer AWS Account Number	The AWS account number-- associated with the AWS account to which software charges are billed
Country	The billin-g address country associated with the AWS account to which software charges are billed
State	The billing address state associated with the AWS account to which software charges are billed
City	The billing address city associated with the AWS account to which software charges are billed
Zip Code	The billing address zip code associated with the AWS account to which software charges are billed
Email Domain	The email domain associated with the AWS account to which software charges are billed, e.g. "amazon.com"
Product Code	A unique identifier for an individual software product
Product Title	The title of the product
Gross Revenue	The amount billed for the usage or monthly fees

Column Name	Description
AWS Revenue Share	The AWS listing fee amount that will be deducted from the billed amount at settlement time
Gross Refunds	The total amount refunded for the transaction (if applicable)
AWS Refunds Share	The portion of the AWS listing fee refunded for the transaction (if applicable)
Net Revenue	The net amount billed for this transaction, less AWS listing fees, refunds, and U.S. sales and use tax
Currency	The currency (e.g. USD)
AR Period	The month and year in which the transaction occurred, in the format "YYYY-MM"
Transaction Reference ID	A unique identifier representing the transaction which can be used to correlate transactions across AWS Marketplace reports
Opportunity Name	The unique identifier for a registered opportunity.
Opportunity Description	Metadata for the registered opportunity.
Solution Title	The name of the solution
Solution ID	The unique identifier for the solution

U.S. Sales and Use Tax Report

This monthly report provides sellers with information about U.S. sales and use taxes collected by Amazon from sales and use transactions in AWS Marketplace. The report only includes products enrolled by sellers in the AWS Marketplace U.S. Sales Tax program.

Publication Schedule

Monthly, on the 15th of the month, by 5:00 PM Pacific Time.

Section 1: US Sales and Use Tax Records

Data Coverage Period

Includes US sales tax amounts resulting from software charges from the previous calendar month.

Column Name	Purpose
Line Item Id	Unique identifier of a line item. Refund transactions have the same Line Item Id as their forward tax transactions
Customer Bill Id	Unique identifier of a customer bill
Product Name	Title of the product purchased
Product Code	A unique identifier representing the individual software product
Product Tax Code	A standard code to identify the tax properties of a product, selected by the seller
Seller Id	Unique identifier of a seller of record for the transaction
Seller Name	The legal name of the seller
Transaction Date	The date of the transaction
Total Adjusted Price	The final price for the transaction
Total Tax	The total tax charged for the transaction
Base Currency Code	This is the base currency code for all AWS Marketplace transactions, which is always USD
Bill to City	The city of the customer's billing address
Bill to State	The state of the customer's billing address
Bill to Postal Code	The postal code of the customer's billing address
Bill to Country	The country of the customer's billing address
Transaction Type Code	The type code of the transaction: AWS, REFUND, TAXONLYREFUND. [See the AWS documentation website for more details] Refund transaction share Line Item Id with their original forward transactions
Display Price Taxability Type	Taxability type for the price displayed to customers. All AWS Marketplace offerings are exclusive
Tax Location Code Taxed Jurisdiction	Vertex Geocode associated with the taxed location
Tax Type Code	Type of tax applied to the transaction. Possible values: None, Sales, SellerUse

Column Name	Purpose
Jurisdiction Level	Jurisdiction level of address used for tax location. Possible values: State, County, City, District
Taxed Jurisdiction	Name of the taxed jurisdiction
Taxable Sale Amount	Amount of transaction that is taxable, by jurisdiction level
Nontaxable Sale Amount	Amount of transaction that is nontaxable, by jurisdiction level
Tax Amount	Tax charged at the jurisdiction level
Tax Jurisdiction Tax Rate	Tax rate applied at the jurisdiction level
Tax Calculation Reason Code	By jurisdiction level, an indicator of whether the transaction is taxable, not taxable, exempt, or zero-rated
Date Used For Tax Calculation	Date used for calculating tax on the transaction
Customer Exemption Certificate Id	Certificate ID representing the exemption certificate
Customer Exemption Certificate Id Domain	This value corresponds to where the certificate is being stored within Amazon systems
Customer Exemption Certificate Level	The jurisdiction level that supplied the exemption
Customer Exemption Code	Code specifying the exemption, e.g. "RESALE"
Customer Exemption Domain	This is the Amazon system that is used to capture the customer exemption information, if any
Customer Reference Id	A unique ID (not AWS Account Number) associated with the AWS account to which fees are billed, to help track usage, revenue, and subscriptions by customers
Transaction Reference Id	A unique identifier representing the transaction which can be used to correlate transactions across AWS Marketplace reports

Daily Ref Tag

This report presents the information from your Marketing Dashboard and provides insight into clicks and conversions for ref tag links that customers use to get to your AWS Marketplace listing.

Publication Schedule

Daily, by 5:00PM PST (UTC -08:00). Covers the previous 24 hour calendar period.

Section 1: Clicks and Conversions

Provides a breakdown of every ref tag used with your products and the amount of clicks, conversions, estimated usage, and estimated revenue associated with them. Here are the data fields for the report:

Columns	Purpose
DATETIME_DAY	Day the ref tag link was first received by our system.
TITLE	Name of the product that.
PRODUCT_CODE	A unique identifier for the product, associated with billing and available in EC2 instance metadata.
ASIN	A unique identifier for your product used in your URL.
REFTAG	Name of the ref tag itself.
CLICKS	Number of visits to page with date, ref tag, and ASIN grouping.
CONVERSIONS	Amount of users who have clicked on the subscribe link on the page after visiting via the ref tag.
USAGE_HOURS	The amount of usage associated with the ref tag.
REVENUE	The estimated revenue from the associated usage. This amount is 'estimated' because customer billing is finalized at the end of each month.

Weekly Ref Tag

This report presents the information from your Marketing Dashboard, summarized by week, and provides insight into clicks and conversions for ref tag links that customers use to get to your AWS Marketplace listing.

Publication Schedule

Weekly, by 5:00PM PST (UTC -08:00). Covers the previous calendar week.

Section 1: Clicks and Conversions

Provides a breakdown of every ref tag used with your products and the amount of clicks and conversions associated with them. Here are the data fields for the report:

Columns	Purpose
TITLE	Name of the product.
PRODUCT_CODE	A unique identifier for the product, associated with billing and available in EC2 instance metadata.
REFTAG	Name of the ref tag itself.
CLICKS	Number of visits to page with date, ref tag, and ASIN grouping.
CONVERSIONS	Amount of users who have clicked on the subscribe link on the page after visiting via the ref tag.

Marketing Your Product

You can contribute to your products' success by driving awareness of AWS Marketplace and by driving traffic directly to the pages on AWS Marketplace where your products are listed for sale. The purpose of this document is to provide the information and support to help you market the product you have listed on AWS Marketplace. Additional information is available in the AWS Marketplace Go-to-Market Program Guide and the AWS Marketplace Go-to-Market Best Practices Guide.

Announcing Your Product's Availability

We encourage you to broadly announce the availability of your product on AWS Marketplace. You may do this via press releases, tweets, blogs, or any other channel you prefer. We've provided sample text that you may wish to include, along with guidelines and instructions for using our trademarks and issuing press releases.

We are happy to review your blogs, tweets and other non-press release announcements prior to going public to ensure consistency with AWS messaging and brand guidelines or voice. Please provide AWS with 10 business days' notice to review and submit to your account manager. Please notify upon posting of any tweets, blogs, and press releases and we will do our best to re-post and increase their visibility.

AWS Marketplace Messaging

In your communications to customers, you may wish to describe the purpose, goals, and benefits of AWS Marketplace. Please see below for standard messaging for AWS Marketplace.

What is AWS Marketplace?

AWS Marketplace is an online store that makes it easy for customers to find, compare, and immediately start using the software and services that run on AWS that they need to build products and run their businesses. Visitors to AWS Marketplace can use AWS Marketplace's 1-Click deployment to quickly launch pre-configured software and pay only for what they use, by the hour or month. AWS handles billing and payments, and software charges appear on customers' AWS bill.

Why would a customer shop on AWS Marketplace?

Finding and deploying software can be challenging. AWS Marketplace features a wide selection of commercial and free IT and business software, including software infrastructure such as databases and application servers, developer tools, and business applications, from popular sellers. AWS Marketplace enables customers to compare options, read reviews, and quickly find the software they want. Once found, they can deploy that software to their own EC2 instance using 1-Click or using the AWS Marketplace Management Console.

Software prices are clearly posted on the website and customers can purchase most software immediately, with payment instruments already on file with Amazon Web Services. Software charges appear on the same monthly bill as AWS infrastructure charges.

Why would software or SaaS providers sell on AWS Marketplace?

With AWS Marketplace, software and Software as a Service (SaaS) providers with offerings that run on AWS can benefit from increased customer awareness, simplified deployment, and automated billing.

AWS Marketplace helps software and SaaS providers that sell software and services that run on AWS find new customers by exposing their products to some of the hundreds of thousands of AWS customers, ranging from individual software developers to large enterprises.

Selling on AWS Marketplace allows ISVs to add hourly billing for their software, without undertaking costly code changes. They simply upload an Amazon Machine Image to AWS and provide the hourly cost. Billing is managed by AWS Marketplace, relieving sellers of the responsibility of metering usage, managing customer accounts, and processing payments, leaving software developers more time to focus on building great software.

Additionally, customers will benefit from the ability to easily deploy preconfigured images of the software simplifying onboarding for new customers.

Linking to AWS Marketplace

Your company likely has a web presence where it describes and promotes your product. We encourage you to highlight the fact that the product is available to run on AWS and can be purchased on AWS Marketplace. To simplify the process for your customers to discover and deploy your software, we have provided instructions for linking your customers to your product.

Using the AWS Marketplace Logo

The **AWS Marketplace** logo is a way to easily tell your customers that your software runs on AWS and is available in AWS Marketplace. If you would like to promote your software in AWS Marketplace, download the logo in .eps (vector) format here.

Linking Directly to Your Product on AWS Marketplace

You can send your customers directly to the product's information page on AWS Marketplace by including deep links on your website or collateral. For web-browser based linking, please use this link structure:

http://aws.amazon.com/marketplace/pp/ASIN/ref=vdr_rf

Replace ASIN segment of the URL with your product's ASIN.

Example:

https://aws.amazon.com/marketplace/pp/B00635Y2IW/ref=vdr_rf

You will find the ASIN in the URL when you search for your application on aws.amazon.com/marketplace. Alternatively, you can consult with your account manager to find the ASIN.

Note: Please test the links before using them to make sure that they direct to the correct page.

Press Releases

As noted above, we encourage you to announce your product's availability on AWS Marketplace through any channel you prefer; however, all press releases that reference AWS Marketplace must be reviewed and signed off by Amazon before any publication or announcement is made. While we encourage you to make announcements, we cannot support joint press releases with AWS Marketplace sellers. We will on a per case review basis support press releases with a quote from AWS if it meets several conditions including but not limited to: it announces a new product or service listed on AWS Marketplace or that it includes a customer reference that uses AWS Marketplace.

All press releases must be drafted by you. We suggest the following headline: [Insert product name] Now Available on AWS Marketplace. Please use the messaging in this document for consistency.

The press release **should**:

- Clearly and accurately describe how the announcement relates to Amazon.com
- Clarify your role on AWS and with customers
- Be customer-focused and emphasize a customer benefit(s)

The press release **should not**:

- Use the terms 'partners' or 'partnership' or 'alliance' to describe the relationship. We prefer 'agreement', 'teamed', or 'relationship'.

- Include a quote from an Amazon Web Services executive unless previously agreed upon
- Include any sales projections; use '.com' by the merchant unless referring to the web site in your company boilerplate
- Refer to your organization as an 'associate' of Amazon.com, as this could be confused with Amazon Associates, our online affiliate program
- Disclose proprietary information about Amazon.com, or refer to our stock ticker symbol. Please submit your press release draft in text format to your account manager.

Review the Amazon Web Services trademark guidelines before using any AWS trademarks. Guidelines specific to the AWS Marketplace trademark are below.

AWS Marketplace Trademark Usage Guidelines

These Guidelines apply to your use of the AWS MARKETPLACE logo and trademark, (each the "Trademark" and collectively the "Trademarks") in materials that have been approved in advance by Amazon.com, Inc. and/or its affiliates ("Amazon"). Strict compliance with these Guidelines is required at all times, and any use of a Trademark in violation of these Guidelines will automatically terminate any license related to your use of the Trademarks.

1. You may use the Trademark solely for the purpose expressly authorized by Amazon and your use must:(i) comply with the most up-to-date version of all agreement(s) with Amazon regarding your use of any of the Trademarks (collectively "Agreements"); (ii) comply with the most up-to-date version of these Guidelines; and (iii) comply with any other terms, conditions, or policies that Amazon may issue from time to time that apply to the use of the Trademark.

2. We will supply an approved Trademark image for you to use. You may not alter the Trademark in any manner, including but not limited to, changing the proportion, color, or font of the Trademark, or adding or removing any element(s) from the Trademark.

3. You may not use the Trademark in any manner that implies sponsorship or endorsement by Amazon other than by using the Trademark as specifically authorized under the Agreements.

4. You may not use the Trademark to disparage Amazon, its products or services, or in a manner which, in Amazon's sole discretion, may diminish or otherwise damage or tarnish Amazon's goodwill in the Trademark.

5. The Trademark must appear by itself, with reasonable spacing between each side of the Trademark and other visual, graphic or textual elements. Under no circumstance should the Trademark be placed on any background which interferes with the readability or display of the Trademark.

6. You must include the following statement in any materials that display the Trademark: "AWS Marketplace and the AWS Marketplace logo are trademarks of Amazon.com, Inc. or its affiliates.

7. You acknowledge that all rights to the Trademark are the exclusive property of Amazon, and all goodwill generated through your use of the Trademark will inure to the benefit of Amazon. You will not take any action that is in conflict with Amazon's rights in, or ownership of, the Trademark.

Amazon reserves the right, exercisable at its sole discretion, to modify these Guidelines and/or the approved Trademarks at any time and to take appropriate action against any use without permission or any use that does not conform to these Guidelines. If you have questions about these Guidelines, please contact ** trademarks@amazon.com** for assistance, or write to us at:

Amazon.com, Inc., Attention: Trademarks

PO Box 81226

Seattle, WA 98108-1226